81
00
1
82
83
84
1
0
86
1
87
90
11
85
90
11
91
92
1
94
96
11

DEMCO

Breathing Tokens

By Carl Sandburg

Abraham Lincoln: The Prairie Years (*Two Volumes*), 1926
Abraham Lincoln: The War Years (*Four Volumes*), 1939
Abraham Lincoln: The Prairie Years and The War Years
    (*One-Volume Edition*), 1954
The Chicago Race Riots, 1919
The American Songbag, 1927
Steichen the Photographer, 1929
Potato Face, 1930
Mary Lincoln: Wife and Widow (*documented by Paul M. Angle*), 1932
Storm Over the Land, 1942
Home Front Memo, 1943
The Photographs of Abraham Lincoln (*with Frederick H. Meserve*), 1944
Lincoln Collector: The Story of the Oliver R. Barrett Lincoln Collection, 1949
Always the Young Strangers, 1953
The Sandburg Range, 1957

NOVEL
Remembrance Rock, 1948

POETRY

Chicago Poems, 1916

Cornhuskers, 1918

Smoke and Steel, 1920

Slabs of the Sunburnt West, 1922

Selected Poems
    (*edited by Rebecca West*), 1926

Good Morning, America, 1928

The People, Yes, 1936

Complete Poems, 1950

Harvest Poems: 1910–1960, 1960

Honey and Salt, 1963

FOR YOUNG FOLKS

Rootabaga Stories, 1922

Rootabaga Pigeons, 1923

Abe Lincoln Grows Up, 1928

Early Moon, 1930

Prairie-Town Boy, 1955

Wind Song, 1960

Edited by

Margaret Sandburg

Carl Sandburg
Breathing Tokens

Harcourt

Brace

Jovanovich

New York

and London

1-81   LA   540

Library of Congress Cataloging in Publication Data

Sandburg, Carl, 1878-1967.
Breathing tokens.

I.   Title.
PS3537.A618B68   1978   811'.5'2   77-85198
ISBN 0-15-114073-1

BCDE

Contents

Portraits

Dune Reflections

Mountain Echoes

Introductory Note

When I first began the work of collecting my father's unpublished poems, one thing was uppermost in my mind—to select, as best I could, only those which he himself would have chosen, and allow those others which I knew he did not want published to repose in the old worn folders. I cannot be sure, of course, that I have done this in all cases, but I have followed what guidelines he left in the notes on some poems, one of which went—"Not to be published until a hundred years after I'm under the sod—but I might change my mind maybe." Nor did I consider any of those which he had in envelopes marked "Indecisive" and "Desperate For Sure."

It was very difficult to make some order out of the chaos in which I found the poems, for handwritten as well as typed copies and carbons, of poems published and unpublished, were in numerous envelopes and folders. But finally I succeeded in separating the published ones from the unpublished—or so I thought at the time. As I went through those that I had considered unpublished, however, I noticed that some had been given more than one title. This became confusing—"Dreaminess Weave," for example, proved to have been published as "Consolation Sonata," and "Men of Science Say their Say" was divided between two published poems, "Call the Next Witness" and "Many Handles." There were many such instances, and they always took me by surprise. (Who would have expected to discover "Soo Line Sonata" in "Lief Ericson"?) I found that I really had to know both the unpublished and the published poems very well indeed to detect these things. Especially since in some instances only the latter part of a poem had been published. In the meantime I was going through a selective process of winnowing out poems that did not seem to fit in with the format I had in mind, or that were too similar to those I knew I would include, or for other reasons. After all this winnowing, I was surprised to find that I had something like two hundred and twenty poems to offer, so that a much larger book than *Honey and Salt* seemed to loom in the offing. In the end, for reasons of space, there had to be a final process of selection.

For invaluable advice and assistance I am deeply indebted to my friend Louise Allen, and for unfailing patience and assistance to Mrs. John Davidson and Mrs. Veronica Currie. Perhaps, too, a note of thanks should be offered here to my sister Helga and her husband, Dr. George Crile, for encouraging me in this project, and to my sister Janet for bearing with me at a time when it seemed about to wear me out.

From the very first, I knew that the title would be *Breathing Tokens*. For although my father has been "under the sod," as he liked to put it, for some years now, here he is again, the old idealist, fighter, philosopher, dreamer, and poet, still with something to say.

MARGARET SANDBURG

Breathing Tokens

Breathing Tokens

1

You must expect to be in several lost causes
 before you die.
Why blame your father and mother for your being
 born; how could they help what they were doing?
And their fathers and mothers farther back? Can we
 say they could help what they were doing?
Why rebuke old barns the wind has not yet blown away?
Why call down anathema on weather lacking ears to hear
 your opinion of it?
Are there historic moments when old Mother Justice, blind-
 folded so she can look and weigh without prejudice
Should make an entry and say with a low contralto of
 pause and finality, "Everybody is wrong and
 nobody is to blame?"

2

 There's no harm in trying.
 Nothing can harm you till it comes.
 And it may never come.
Or if it comes it is something else again.
And those who say, "I'll try anything once,"
often try nothing twice, three times,
arriving late at the gate of dreams worth dying for.

3

Be a leopard: set aside six minutes a day: count your spots.
 Try rubbing out the spots: see how it works.
 Write box car numbers on the white spots.
 Put sevens and elevens on the black spots.
 Say out loud, "I am a Numbah One Leopard—
"I was not born a two spot: hear me, heeyah me, I am Numbah One."
Of course, Mistah Man, this is out of your class.
You are not so silly as to sit counting your spots.
You would not be saying, "Heeyah me, I am Numbah One."

Or be a giraffe and say:
"This neck is beyond question to identify me if I get lost"
Or: "My necklength is fixed by law and is therefore proper."
Yes be a giraffe: you got a right to try it.
Look down longnecked on those born shortnecked.
Chew the choice leaves of trees: tell others to eat grass.
Of course, Mistah Man, you draw elegant distinctions.

4

Be a zebra: wear stripes
Cultivate the sport model look.
Let others place their bets on whether you are
a white jackass with black stripes or vice versa.
Wear anything you want to wear.
Or wear what everybody is wearing.

Be the father of five alligators, five sharks.
Teach the little ones to take care of their teeth
and the value of teeth in earning a living.

Or be born, if you can, among the swift fish.
Learn how to go over and under, sidewise, zigzag.
Let the sliding of a snake on its belly be a lesson.
Study the elephant: he considers it an honor to eat hay
and to kill only when some killer comes to kill him.
He addresses the aggressor: "Why bother me? I warned you
                                        not to bother me."

Try being a goat: put on a face of calm contemplations.
Look people in the eye as though unaware they gaze at you.
Read their innermost hidden secrets.
Then turn away toward other horizons chewing your cud.
How should their sins and prides be anything to you?
What have they learned of alfalfa and soy bean hay
or the somersaults of kids born for acrobatics?

5

Be a bottle: say glug-glug: be a clock: say tick-tock.
Study why the clock never glugs
and why the bottle might try telling time and fail.
Consider the origins of men saying horsefeathers
                                    yes horsefeathers.

6

Inquire into the monotony of shirts soiled
going to the laundry and returning to be soiled,
how each proud man is every so often sent to the cleaners,
how the bottle sellers rejoice over news of broken bottles.

Inquire further into the high contrasts
between those who can eat glass and like it
and connoisseurs who require bottled velvet,
and fixity of one living oceanic squid
and flights of those who are born birds.
Shall the squid have praise or blame for being a squid?
Shall the bird have compliments for being born with wings?
    What shall a broken bottle
    tell a brand new bottle?
    "Your time will come—
          you'll get yours"
          something like that?

7

Be what you want to be.
An oak, a blossom, a dry leaf in the wind
or the wind blowing the dry leaf; or both.
Be a gong or three gongs in one: a gong of silence:
A gong of clamor crying hellsbells to the satisfied:
A gong of smooth songs saying yes and welcome.

Be what an earthworm means to be
in the measure of its circumference
so humble so slow so true
to the date of the stars it was born under.

Your personal doorways know your shadows
and number the times you enter, exit, enter
so often having no lines to say
though you are actor and audience to yourself.

Thrust laughter from your diaphragm whensoever.
Be perpendicular till the finish.
You will be horizontal long enough afterward
with toes shoving up the daisies
yielding to the earth's ancient mulch.

8
Be ice: be fire.
Be hard and take the smoothing of brass for your own.
Be sensitized with winter quicksilver below zero.
Be tongs and handles: find breathing tokens.
See where several good dreams are worth dying for.

Nocturnes
and Sketches

Journal Note Long Ago

Crossing the wilderness or the sea I take with me nobody
who is afraid nor do I want with me the memory of a man
or woman who is afraid.

I am afraid enough myself now—there are shadows and ghosts
enough now—in the meshes of my corpuscles—and so I must
not ask others to go.

I keep the memory of a dog who was never afraid, a wagon
whose wheels lasted, a child who had not lived long enough
to know the meaning of the words Yesterday and Tomorrow.

1914

White Dancer

Birches shone white on a point of land
    in a lake in north Minnesota.
The moon came with a shine of white added
    where the birches shone on a point of land
    far in the north in Minnesota.
The winter snow came adding a shine of white
    to the birches and the moon.
The ghost of a blond woman came dancing in a white
    sheet in the birches, the moon, the winter snow.
A line of red on her mouth, a circle of red at her
    hair, two spots of red at her ankles,
The ghost of a blond woman came dancing among birch
    moon snows of winter white in Minnesota far
    north in Minnesota.

1915

Nocturne I

Not one slow motion in the long coal boat,
It waits in the dark among the spider shadows
Twisting into the moonrays quivering near the walls.

The tall lean skyscraper on the lake front
Looks across to red lights running the harbor
Reaching a dark head through the smoke amid the whispers
                    of the stars.

Lake waters off the east lunge lazy at the piers.
Purple shawls of night play around a tug hustling in.
Strips of gray and yellow move to the hunched shoulder
Of an excursion barge heavy with a murmur of many voices
                    laughing and singing.

Bronzed Grackles

In the home of the bronzed grackles now there is peace.
The bronze on the necks of the grackles shines and shimmers,
Fades and fools on the slide of the feathers.
They sleep and there is ease in the home, ease and peace.
The fire of the sun, the wet of the rain,
The open and climbing clouds of white up the south and west,
They sit and see these, feeling bronze on their necks
With the hoarse understanding of grackles.

Journey and Oath

When Abraham Lincoln received a bullet in the head
    and was taken to the Peterson house across the
    street,
He passed on and was swathed in emulsions and pre-
    pared for a journey to New York, Niagara, across
    Ohio, Indiana, back to Illinois—

As he lay looking life-like yet not saying a word,
Lay portentous and silent under a glass cover,
Lay with oracular lips still as a winter leaf,
Lay deaf to the drums of regiments coming and going,
Lay blind to the weaving causes of work or war or peace,
Lay as an inextinguishable symbol of toil, thought, sacrifice—

There was an oath in the heart of this man and that:
    By God, I'll go as a Man;
    When my time comes I'll be ready.
    I shall keep the faith that nothing
      is impossible with man, that one
      or two illusions are good as money.
    By God, I'll be true to Man
    As against hog, louse, fox, snake, wolf,
    As against these and their counterparts
      in the breast of Man.
    By God, I'll fight for Man
    As against famine, flood, storm,
    As against crop gambling, job gambling,
    As against bootlickers on the left hand,
    As against bloodsuckers on the right hand,
    As against the cannibalism of the exploitation
      of man by man,
    As against insecurity for the sanctities of
      human life.

1915

Others
Fantasia for Muskmelon Days

Ivory domes . . white wings beating
    in empty space . .
Nothing doing . . nuts . . bugs . . a regular
    absolute humpty-dumpty business . .
    pos-i-tive-ly . . falling off walls
    and no use to call doctor, lawyer,
    priest . . no use, boy, no use.

O Pal of Mine, O Humpty Dumpty,
    shake hands with me.
O Ivory Domes, I am one of You:
        Let me in.
      For God's sake—let me in.

Sand Writing

Does the sea forgive, forget or remember?
Write on the sand and see how the white
    horses ride over and leave no names,
    no almanac days, on the beach.
Write six wrongs on the sand and watch
    the sea wall fall on them.

1909

I Know They Sleep Well

White winter stars
In the bowl of sky,
I find you many more
in the bowls of the sea.

Slivers of the red morning sun,
You too I find many more
In the bowls of the sea.

The sea,
the clear, clean sea
doubles and redoubles
One white winter star,
one sliver of the sun . .
. . I know they sleep well.

I know they sleep well
in the sea and the sun.

One ship, ten, a hundred,
and the men and the women
in the gag of the salt and wet.

One ship, ten, a hundred,
and steel that steers and whines
straight for a hole in a hull

I know they sleep well
and the tooth of a shark is clean
and the bones are clean
on the old sea-floor . . where . .
I know they sleep well.

In No-Man's land
the sun has a chance
at the dummies that dangle
humped and huddled on wires.

Let only the sun and the rain
Eat and play at the wires
and there will be . .
. . only ghost dummies huddling.

It's a stuttering song
and mumbles its meanings . .
. . I know they sleep well.

1916

From an Illinois Prairie Hut

For Amy Lowell

She regrets a lost town in Vermont,
lost streets of her childhood town in Vermont;
grassroots tugging at the streets and taking Main Street
of her childhood town, the old home town, in Vermont,
     these she regrets,
     and each regret is a grassroot
     and a grassroot must be strong and bitter.

She regrets a horse chestnut,
a tree with a torso ten people join hands and circle round,
a buckeye dying, a tough and beautiful horse chestnut dying,
she regrets this storm of white blossoms will not paint the summer
    sky when the buckeye is gone—
     and each regret
     is a high thin goose of autumn
     crying south, crying south.

She fixes the millimeters of her glasses herself;
She measures the curve of her eyesight wishing to measure
The curve of the arch of the sky of night, the curve of the
    running hours on the level of night,
And the moon stumbles of early morning and the testimony of
    the dawn across the first light sheets.
She measures the millimeters of her eyesight with regrets
     and each regret is a grassroot
     and each regret is a high thin goose of autumn crying
     south.

Louis Mayer's Ice Pictures

"Icy Shores"

Why has the sea hurled itself on the land
Now that summer is gone
And winter is the big player?
                          Neither is the winner.
Both strugglers, sea and land,
Are locked in a standstill.
Only the ice is a victim.
It happened to be caught between.
So the ledges are crumpled . . . broken playthings.
They are equal to a toy town of blocks
Kicked over by children
Who are gone away.

"Walrus Bay"

High banks with a hard feel to them
Stand up from a slow plash of gray waves.
Humped rocks too
And looking twice at the humped rocks
We see they are not walrus playing tag
As we guessed at first.
No life of blood, throat and nostril
Runs under them; they are granite
Heaved up years ago to companion the sea.

"Solitude"

I can have this cool loneliness
And you can take along what you want
Here of this cool loneliness.

It is not like prairie land
Nor a single crag
Nor a level of ocean.
Little hills around it
Keep off winter,
The big rough player.
A disc of cool loneliness,
I always ask it:
What are you waiting for?
It seems so sure somebody is coming.

— Others, March 1916

You and a Sickle Moon

The lips of you are with me tonight.
And the arms of you are a circle of white.

The dream of it burns.
And I want you and the stars.
I want you and a sickle moon.

The finger tips of you
Five hundred miles away
Make a wireless crying flash:
I know a search that's useless,
I know a code I don't hunt for,
I know a face that's gone.

Back home the hills talk to me.
Here the hills are strangers.

The lips of you are a ghost.
The arms of you are a ghost.
    The red and white is empty air.

Omaha 1917

21

Prayer for the Child Margaret Who Is Six

This is an intercession to you, O God,
Who are the God men mean when they cry
"God help us all!"

To you, O God, I enter this plea;
Let this child be not too literal.
Let her take twice two as four, the unchangeable fact,
Yet give her the freedom, the equilibrium,
White wings (you know what I mean, God).

Let her suspect on a Black Friday
When a high wind piles sheep wool on a blue sky
That two and two may be five or three and a half.
Let her have enough formulas for computations
And after that, shuffle mathematics as her little hands
Now shuffle the white spots on the black dominoes
Of the pieces face down, mysterious, unbeknown,
In the boneyard.

Let it sink into her heart, O God,
How the prairie face is eaten by the slow fire of the sun
And how the orioles warble all summer
And when they go they go humbly,
Because they must go,
With six or seven easy sunset songs.
And the best way is the beautiful singing way.

Let the truth of Jack and the Beanstalk enter her mind
Equally true with the location of the postoffice
Because a beanstalk whereon a washerwoman's son
May climb above the clouds,
Is so impossible, it will train her soul
For the great impossibilities,

The great loves, the hates that nourish better than milk,
The destiny of her shapely forearms when they are written
among the Karnak hieroglyphics will belong with
the memories and ashes of forms that took the
copper wash of the winter sunset for a hair
ribbon color.

1917

Death Is a Dream Woman

Death is a dream woman.
Her fingers bring flowers of twilight.

Death in her fingers keeps cool dreams.
She touches an eyelid and a fighting man loosens his fists
She touches a mouth and a gold lady's lips are molten:
> they soften as copper to fire when Death
> says, "Hush thee, my babbie."

I know the old dream woman has songs somewhere
In pawn with rhythms of fiddlers and dancers
Kept for the lockers of ash, or grey, of twilight ashen grey.

She mixes dust and dawn to a bread and the eaters tell no
> news; they keep their passwords, friends let
> into a sacrament.

She fixes a dish of dreams, Death does, and pours it into the
> dusk and stars, pours it for children, for
> chattering sparrow children.

Nocturne II

They circle and reach,
Fixed in the whirling feet
Of fire dancers, gipsy women,
Early in their twenties,
Learning,
Early with a smolder of sun
In their eyes and the skin of their cheekbones.

Did I say words?
Love? Death? Money?
And they are liars?

I know nothing.
I know only what the night knows.
I know the night's pearl grey
Of the Hudson River from Grant's Tomb;
I know the salt wash klug-klug, ka-lug-ka-lug.
And near morning suspects of dawn
Fluttering a near silver on the east roofs.

Lights out of the steep hills:
            you are cities at a standstill.
Lights out of the river:
            you are boats, sleeping, working,
            winning salt arcs of the earth,
            tossing hello to Liverpool, Hong Kong.

Flame lines out of pearl and grey,
Singing ka-lug-ka-lug out of the salt wash,
Silver slivers on the east roofs:
            I have forgotten many.
            I remember you.

Evening Landscapes in Your Eyes

Evening landscapes in your eyes,
Evening, dusk, and the march of stars.
    The hoot owl call lingers across the blossoms.
    A light wind shakes a snow of blossoms down.
Only early June and the lilac mist deepens.
The scars of the japonica redden.
    Sunsets dwindle, stars blink—it is none of these,
    Not one of all moving slow in shadows across
    The evening landscapes in your eyes.

Dawn-shot

They use the rose of Sharon to speak of women.
They use the lily and the pansy for metaphors.
They tell us about pools and the sea and stars.

I am hunting you somewhere else.
I am hunting a spear-gray, dawn-shot horizon.
I am hunting a spear-red, swimming sunset.

Chinese Letters or Korean
From a Window

One time the moon whitened the fields, whitened the
          pastures, polished the floor for the dancers;
Let the dancers foot it, earth, legs to the moon,
Look up at the face of the moon and laugh with their
          laughter—
Silver mist, yellow mist, grey mist of dawn,
Eyes open, eyes closing, tell me, did they once lose
          a beat in the measures?—
And let a long brown horse nose to the ground go eating
          tufts of moonshine, go walking from tree
          to proud tree in the ballroom.

                    · ·

The moon laughs at these streets.
The tongues of sea mist creep and lick and wind
And say to the trillion lights
A wet night leaves your city—

                    · ·

Those who look from a ten story window
Cannot look up at the moon and laugh—
They look out through a lane between bricks over ships,
Widening into a pasture of stars
          above Long Island.
They cannot look up at the moon and laugh.
Their eyes meet the gaze of the moon and catch her high laughter.
"Yes with my gold paint brush I am painting your hotel sky
Immemorial blue, lapis lazuli sky.
But you, though you try and try
May not even touch with your fingers the blue of my sky—
Looking in at your window of bricks
I laugh and laugh again
          Hearing you cry."

Writings Left by a Guitar Player Who Wished to Live One More Winter

Child of the rich red mouth,
come to me and tell me
how you grew in the wild grass,
how you and your children came,
how the lights in your eyes grew,
how kisses were taken and yet
kisses grew richer and redder.
Tell me how the years left you
younger.

* * *

The gold axis of the sun
accomplishes miracles.
Stand on the railroad track
where the rails run into the sun,
measure the gold, the axis,
take it home,
and measure the miracle.

* * *

Old wood from China
must be fixed over.

Old pictures from Korea,
old stories of silk threads
changing into a roomful of butterflies
and changing back again for a miracle,
all must be fixed over.

* * *

Meditations on old Japanese lutes
come out with finger thrummings.
Notes picked off with wise fingers
jump into the air as fairy acrobats
sent out to do and be done.

* * *

The winter birds are few
and their songs are few.

Hiding out from the hunting winds
They defeat the hunt of the winds.

Saying "orioles are few now" is wrong
because there are no orioles at all now.

There is a mousey grey wind people, nevertheless,
short dwarf birds chasing starved morsels;
they get by where orioles strangle.

Even if the winter birds are few,
little and strong they beat their hunters;
sometimes they chuckle hungry to sleep.

Any Blue-Jay Knows How

There is a special flutter of your hand sometimes
Leaping from your side to the sleeve of my fore-arm.
Any blue-jay in the third week of May
When the lilacs break for the sun
Knows how: any blue-jay
Clamoring from the river-shine
One to the red-haw blossoms . . .
Any blue-jay knows how.

One memory a-flutter again:
A yellow shoulder among white stones.
A yellow shoulder telling the sea heart-things.

Say . . keep it under your hat.
Say . . keep it under your lashes.
. . . And tell me again
How the white stones were clean,
How the line of the sea spoke.
And how the yellow shoulder remembers.

Only Names

Whether it is a dog star or a plow star
Climbing the northern ridges over the coffee pot,
Whether it is a white clover or a blue clover
Marching on the meadows of the ponies,
The names of the stars and flowers for you and me
Are only names, are only broken syllables, after all.

   Over the meadow ponies,
Over the ridges and clover,
A spray of a hundred stars and one red star,
And the red star does not know my name,
And the red star does not know your name,
And you—and I—do not know the star's name.
It is a dog star or a plow star
Climbing the ridges over the coffee pot.
It is a star you and I will remember,
And the meadows and ponies will remember.

Shooting Stars Can Sing

The patches of shooting stars next to the railroad track
Come out singing in May, singing in pink and white.

Or is it singing? Or do they guess how other people come by
To speak and believe a patch of shooting stars can sing?

The rains come up out of the east
Blowing pearls over the leaves;
The rains go down, the sun hauls
Old wagons spilling over a silver
On the pink and white; night opens
The old doors for keeping wagons;
Drips of starlight fall, fall.

Among the patches of shooting stars next to the railroad track
There is a program, first this, then that, opening and closing
      numbers.

Commuter Pioneers

Knock me down with a feather, carissima.
This is a time for foolish things.
Our next-door neighbors are painting the house pink
And I believe they are going to boil ham
And start out next Sunday on a green grass picnic;
Even last night they were singing:
                "And the green grass grew all around."
Phenoms checkered with these loud colors
Fill me with the sea voices of my own enigmas.
It is wrong for me to sit at the window looking on
And wiggling my ears with amusement at these April gypsies,
Commuters with the instincts of prairie pioneers,
Frying grouse in a late prairie sunset,
Eating fried grouse under the early prairie stars:
I tell you these things get into my system too
And I feel like buying a hunk of salami
And five bottles of beer.

Sunday Afternoon or Theorems in White

Moonlight on young corn,
shifting in a soft green sea
    of southwest breezes idling over Illinois,
A farmhand jimmying the keys of an accordion
    for waltzers of the old fashioned dances
    on a long porch between portals of milk cans,
And cross-lights, streaming cross-lights along the
    slants of prairie, tossed triangles of motor
    lights on a white pike in the white moon—
Can I tie these in a bundle and bundle them on to you?
Can I lay these leaf on leaf for you and send them on?
I met up with these last night. And today I met up with:
                    catalpa blossoms
            swaying in the breeze, blossom
            masses: the top of the summer,
            the high hunch of the hills of
            summer and then down, the big
            white cry before it's all over,
            the long low-sung breath—the
            mother catalpa sending its armies
            of children whitening more and more
            the pike already white in the moon—
—Why should I? I didn't have to. There was no law, no ordinance of
the village, no order from the government nor the high men of the
books—I caught a handful of falling blossoms, five white leaves writ-
ten on, written with whispers from the deepest sap and root of the big-
armed branching mother catalpa
            —I threw five white blossom leaves into a bowl of
spring water—and I sat and read them over and over, spray fingers of
vermilion maroon lines spread how, which, when—finger prints from
far down—vermilion maroon bronze hair of marching whispering un-
known children—the winds and the waters blew them here to the
tremulous mystic blossom leaves

  —I shall wait long before I tell anybody anywhere about it—unless you already know the password how can I give it to you—I leave it to you to sit an hour and an hour on a Sunday afternoon with blossoms, listening to the thin music spray of white—they dance their own dances, flyers down a white pike in a white moon.

Heaven Is a Valley of Cool Timber

Hush, mouths of mist: whisper it:
Say it with goat-crooked ankles
Moving where a horse-tooth crops new grass.
Blur this night, blur the white fog walls.
The railroad trains cross and plunge.
The headlights fix lost bayonets in the white fog walls.
The white fog opens, the fog walls close.
The moan of the six-eight wheels on the spikes and rails
Is the grind of a cello bow on a low down string.

      Hush, gray stars: hush, Oh treetops.
      Heaven is a valley of cool timber.

Blue smoke plume, burr oak embers,
Be good to us: warm our hands and feet.
The headlights cross and cross to the white fog walls.
The fog yawns for its children: mother fog, they are yours.
Hush, gray stars: you too be good to us: let us read
Your oldest lantern writings, your scraggly alphabets:
Put us wise, gray stars, us of the rushing hands and feet
Running to you some night like the rushing railroad trains,
One and another and another into the white fog.

      Hush, gray stars: hush, Oh treetops.
      Heaven is a valley of cool timber.

The wagons pass, the wagons home with corn.
Corn, yellow corn to the tops of the wagons,
Home they go, loaded to the wagon shoulders,
Loaded like shouldering workmen the wagons go in the dusk.
The gypsies sit by the roadside; the police took their bear away.
"If only the bear came back," the gypsies sit wishing a wish
For the climbing bear, the bear who shinned up a telegraph pole
And sat on the cross-arms playing a mouth organ.
"Come back, Oh bear," the red bandannas cry: the wagons pass:
The headlights slide into the white fog: night lives on:

Hush, gray stars: hush, Oh treetops.
Heaven is a cool timber valley
Heaven is wagons and a lost bear.

Chariots clash on the roads to heaven.
The high hard hubs of the chariots swear and laugh.
Over the white fog the chariots lift and swing.
Laugh if you want to: laugh here: these are the wheels
And drivers who sang first "Swing low, sweet chariot."
These are the chariots that never were, these are the mystic,
The lost impossible chariots: this is the heart of a gypsy
When a bear is lost.

Hush, gray stars: hush, Oh treetops.
Heaven is a cool valley of timber
Heaven is a heart of lost chariots.

1920

37

River Town Equations

On the sea-green corn
the wind drove sea-horses—
silver whips, you tire like
   the sea tires, never at all—
The corntassels keep it up all
    day—the corn, the sea, the
    wind, are family relations.

      . .

Fields in the town
and fields outside
the same river knows you,
the same rains.

      . .

The river loafs,
Six arches loaf,
   And the bridges steady
   and steer their curves
   and stand to the load,
Main Street bridge for the wagons,
The railroad bridge for the Omaha hummer.

      . .

The river stops
to be hitched for a work horse
when the power dam says so.
   River and power dam chuckle together:
   Look who we are, we are the grinders,
   Who's gonna do your grindin' when we are gone?
The miller writes on his sacks, "Belle Flour Mills."

The sheets of the power dam sunset lights
Lift from a rust and a blood to a lit maroon,
To a series of seven yellow sisters.

  . .

The prairie brown grass runs.
The up-river slants to a hill mass,
To corntop hills and hills of hickory.

  . .

Between a corntop hill and a hickory timber,
Look twice . . for a shy graveyard.
Look twice . . and maybe you sing:
Hunt for my grave after I die—hide my bones
      in a blue mist tomb.

  . .

And yet,—I am no proud man today.
I saw the clam shovelers
Knee deep in the loafing river
Sifting the water in their sifting shovels,
Picking the white shell mussels,
Picking the pink shell mussels,
Buttons for shirts and pajamas,
Buttons for picnics, weddings, jobs,
Buttons for the yama-yama polka-dot shirt-tail
    parade of the wriggling bones
      to a blue mist tomb.

I said it—I am no proud man.
I am a little brother of buttons, clams, diggers,
I have seen the knee-deep diggers sifting the water
    in their sifting shovels.

Hunt for my grave after I die—hide my bones in a
   blue mist tomb.

                  • •

The eyes in a buffalo head are strong and sad,
The great long curve of the river is strong and sad.

The feel of an Indian stone pot-scraper is smooth.
The way this river works south is smooth.

Whatever the sky says the river throws it back.

                  • •

The White Horse Inn is gone.
A faded sign on a faded house.
   Tell me at the doorstep here some story.
   Tell me two men shot each other for a woman.
   Tell me they hanged a horsethief here.
   Tell me a woman burned as a witch here.
Tell me anything about this ground I stand on here.
I believe anything if it is old enough.
I am the child who knows how history comes from the
   babbling tongues.

                  • •

In the county jail I heard the jailbirds harmonizing.
"We're going home, no more to roam," mocking barbershop
   chords, men who spit on the law, runaway boys,
   runaways learning.
Evening cheepers, watchers of the dusk in the maples
   watching the jail,
They heard, and I heard, unconquerable barbershop chords.

                  • •

There was a hummer mumbled by
on a humble mumbling bridge,
the evening Omaha hummer.

. .

The motor cars snort
and toss their triangles of crossed lights
to the dip of the Main Street bridge and over,
to the highway spans and the hickory hills.

The conquering shaft of this funnel,
the light conquering Main Street,
the crash of these conquering wheels—
this is the overland limited interurban—
this makes no stops between here and Chicago.

And yet—I, who am no proud man,
I know the copper face men had a village here,
ran in moccasins, ran thirty miles a day overland,
ran and sang, Oh Silver Face, to the white rim moon
      I see tonight.

. .

In front of the court-house was a statue whispering: Victory.
    In the light of the mystical moon I saw it,
    In the whispering silver mist
I did not fathom or understand its meaning at all.
It was somebody twisted from a day-shape to a night-shape
In the haze of the twisting moon night silver,
Twisted to stand and look at the corntop hills, the old
      night river,
Whispering to the blue night: Victory,
Whispering, "Especially ask the marvelous fields"—
Over and over whispering, "Especially ask the marvelous
      fields."

Shasta Transcriptions

1

Let the tall rain-soaked hemlock look down.
Let the pools of light take the torso of the hemlock
     and hold it in this pink and silver sunset.
Let the lights stack and dwindle, repeat, foregather,
     and shove out one by one alone.
Let them have this altar service as ordered.

2

"Like a father, like a child."
So Shasta stands, so Shasta glitters.

Wings fill the sky on Puget Sound.
White wings count up on the gray field.
They dip and fly with the sheep-gut twists
     of the Southern Pacific up the Siskiyou,
     as the logs come down the cut at
     Chuckanute—
As Shasta glitters in her Judgment Day robes.

Will I climb one of those red bastions
     and there wait and straddle a white wind
     to ride, ride, ride?

Now I have seen the little armies of the sundown
     go marching, go moving, go maneuvering.
I have listened almost to the little droning drums
     of their dwindling dreams.

I saw that shining blackhawk.
Maybe I shall wheel over those slopes in a long curve
     alone with a shining blackhawk.

Will I climb up one of those last few red
      bastions and there wait and straddle a white wind
      to ride, ride, ride?

Valley of Bitter Tears

I saw her go over the mountain
and in the valley spoken of so often
as a valley of bitter tears.

I saw her shoulder as a shadow,
a little gaunt line against sunset lights,
and the way she was going was over the mountain,
over and down to the valley of bitter tears.

The rain came once to that valley,
slanting marches of beating rain,
and that was a million years ago,
and the rain there now is only bitter tears.

And when I have made a picture,
or when I have made a song,
I often see the mountain,
I often see her shoulder,
I see her going down to the valley of bitter tears,
a little gaunt line against the sunset lights.

Night Will Come Again

Night of course will come again,
one old friend saying, "I come ever ever
and I teach you the meaning of ever ever:
Bring me one of your griefs
and see whether I can lose it for you:
time and again I have taken a fierce grief
and shaded it to a lesser sorrow."
Yes night without fail will come again,
the same night we saw move
in maroon lengths up Tuolumne Canyon,
the same other night we saw bend with stars
and fold with mist and become a finespun rain
you met with a running light laughter.
In this night yes now walk again
and see how your tears are kin to its mist,
your freegiven tears I saw:
my guess goes with yours: night is better yet
for teaching us how to say ever ever.

Study in Mountain Copper

> In a red canyon
> White waters run.
The foam is a feathery flicker.
A woman's face slides on the bubbles.
The sun comes west and shadows turn runaway.
> > The red walls
> > and white waters
> > burn.
The woman's face keeps sliding on the bubbles,
> a Red Indian face.
The foam is a flicker of red feathers.

Mule

I give you the mule, a silhouette on the horizon, his long ears forming
points of shadow individual and all by themselves.

He is passing out somewhere, his work done he is leaving the stage
like an old actor with a cracked voice superseded by a young one
whose speech is faultless.

Write on the tomb of the mule, on the one vast historic repository
containing all that remains of the mule these words:

I builded railroads and I fought wars and I changed the land from a
broken wilderness to a country filled with cities and crossed with
rails; hitched to the iron scoops and shovels I dug the paths of
civilization or whatever you call the thing you now have: now vast
mules of steel, snorting steam and eating coal take my place; they
obey more and they love less than I did the human hands that feed
them.

Aztecs

I know the Aztecs were glad.
I know the Aztec women threw themselves away.
I know the Aztec men lost their heads.
I know the Aztecs.
I am an old Aztec myself.
How else could I show the Aztecs for
      what they were and are?
I shall be an Aztec again.

. . .

Shining woman, did he give you
      a pair of golden shoes?
Did he find you a thin soft cloth
      of gold for your arches and ankles?

Sea Music

The silver foam of this sea music sinks into several
              deaths.
The first of the deaths sits in a golden saddle and
              is shod with amethyst, the first is a
              little too loud.
The seventh comes on a foot of whisper wings—it is
              hardly to be heard.

The Sag

I have heard the great green earth and the gray stars on a dew-dripping summer night, I have heard them breathe.

I slept on a hilltop in the Sag valley.

I slid that day down yellow dirt roads of hills that gave no warning; five hills in a half-mile non-committal as a gray-eyed woman; five slopes with the jaws of hold-up men on a winter midnight; I tore through the ruts a toboggan pace; I slid with my toes on a coaster-brake.

The open night and the open sky—was it a mother-woman or a girl-child?

An outpour of simple and equal mysteries. The moon was silver at eight o'clock. The moon was yellow at eleven. It was blood-red dropping good-by down a blue timber rim at one o'clock.

Sleep is a lover of mine and all night other lovers came and would not let sleep finger my eyelids. All night one lover and another with story and song cry.

The catbird chuzzled a short thin sob. It was a feather of cry. One-two-three and no more of it.

The bones of my knees, young as the wheeling constellations, shook in an army blanket. I lay on my back, two hands under my neck. Shooting stars warmed me. Bingo! plim-plim! and they slid down the sky-ways. Five white shooting stars in the north and the east, in the night and the morning. Tongue-flashes that said, "Here we go! and hurrah for the next who goes!" I was chilled and they warmed me.

The hill was a bald-headed hill, an old and a grizzled pal, and it heaves to a watching moon, it heaves to a changing Dipper, it knows the first names of the Seven Sisters, the bald-headed hill could have held ten thousand boys under army blankets.

Three notes of a whip-poor-will; three times over and three times over; it was made out of running water in the starlight; it was made in the gloaming of silver leaves in a moonlit timber; it is a night-whim of God; three times over and three times over.

Dew: a wet gray on the leather saddle, an added nickel on the handle-bars. Dew: a shawl and a cape for the ash and the oak. Dew: a line and a film down two miles of the Sag.

The trees sleep and wake and nod in the wind their heavy heads and heavy shoulders and then go back to sleep. The grass sleeps first and last and hears nothing; the grass knows much; the grass knows how to wait.

Dancing girls? Long white arms in a scarf dance? slowly and mournfully forty Ophelias? No—only the pool-mist of old quarries, old gashes of limestone in the Sag.

Try the midnight cry of a mule for loneliness. Listen alone on a hilltop to the ancient pain and joy and want of a mule in a wooded pasture, the hee and the haw of a hoarse wish calling under long ears to five shooting stars.

Whose warble? Six sliding architectural notes. A thousand years the tribe sings it so. A thousand years the six notes slide from the throat so. And who cares under the shooting stars of a summer night for a thousand years?

It is a mate call: I love and I love and I will go on loving to the end.

It is a mother-call to a child with wrong dreams: quiet, child, quiet, for the night is young and the sun comes and the dark is gone, and mother and the moon give you kisses.

These are the six notes that slid on a summer night from a tree in the Sag valley to a hilltop and two ear drums and a garrulous fluting memory.

. . .

Deeper than the nickel on the handle-bars one star keeps the east and the other stars are players quitting the field for a game that is over; one star shines on; the light tells numbers on the face of a ticking watch; it is time for a fire and a pot of coffee; it is early morning.

Across the valley roosters and one cheer for each of the gone stars, one cheer for a ribbon of sun. Across the valley crows hurling a red hunger of cries against the lavender sunrise.

I was a nothing and a nobody passing that way for a night. The valley sang its home-songs for itself. The shooting stars spilled their streaks of fire for themselves. The play of the moon and the birds and the white-armed pool-mist was the same the night before I came and the night after. I was the listener who came to sleep and never slept at all and was glad.

I have heard the great green earth and the gray stars on a dew-dripping summer night, I have heard them breathe.

I remember the Sag with a garrulous fluting memory.

Portraits

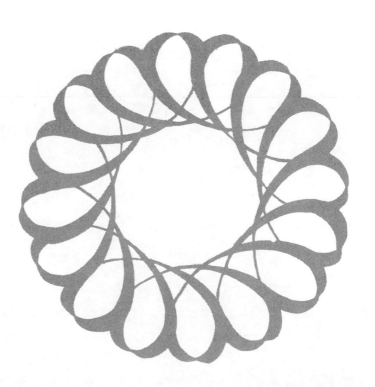

To a Poet

You said I would go alone,
I would find my way.
But you were the strongest person I had known.
You were the morning wind, and you were stone.
You said; I know that you will go your way.
Whatever horse you want to ride is yours,
And night is yours, and the evening gleams, and day.
I can tell you nothing you have not known.
I said; I go with you; I am your own.
But I went alone.

An Old Woman
For My Mother

Looking on the open
Glow of a full-golden moon
In the drowsy, almost noiseless
Dream-watch peace of midnight
In a prairie town, she
Touched me with her lips and hands
and babbled softly she would
Listen till the sound of my footsteps
Was gone.

I kissed my hand to the dim shape
Standing in the shadows under the porch
Looking good-by to her boy
And I keep a picture
Of one shaft of moonlight
Trembling near her face
Telling of wishes farther than love or death,
The infinite love of an old woman
Keeping a hope for her boy.

Letter to Paula from a Hill Near Croton

Paula:
I pick this for you
on a hill near Croton.
The evening lights of Sing Sing
flicker a brass bar . .
. . a living gold wire of light . .
a flickering strip of hot gold . .
down among rock-walled hills of the Hudson.
"There" says John Reed and his right forefinger,
"is the point of land where André met Benedict Arnold"
"and" says the shifting forefinger
"straight across the river is West Point."
(And an Illinois boy's head flutters:
Grant, Lee, Gettysburg, Zachary Taylor, Chapultepec,
The Rio Grande, Pershing, Toul, Cantigny:
A boy's head flutters with names.)
"And that is Haverstraw":
Another gold wire of molten light
Laid quivering on a weave of shadows,
hill rock and night river nets of dusk.
    A great moon pours silver here
    where the feet of Isadora Duncan
    dreamt new dances . .
and the Sing Sing, Haverstraw wires of molten light
quiver at the night's questions.

Marny

Smolder of dreams in your slow, proud eyes,
Flicker of roses maroon in your shadows of hair,
You, the youngblood, the lightfoot,
Took the road and went away to find answers
Unto the words unanswerable.
You lay before us when we, for tears,
Held our lips and could not tell you how dreams and roses go
                                    and where.

Your proud eyes hunting the answers,
Your hair and roses of shadow and maroon,
Mixing in the dusk down the great road you took,
    You found the gulches and the ashes,
    Saw rain drive lonely on the marshes,
    Patrols of star and moon cross the sky
    And purple, drifting nocturnes.

                                    1936

Portrait of a Colyumnist

He might have been a jockey
Wearing a yellow cap
And a yellow silk shirt.

Facing a Blickensderfer typewriter
He improvises jokes and gibes
With a don't-care hurdy-gurdy
Slant of the head.

And he says, "Hello, stranger"
With a Texan ease
And a light of the eyes—
He might be straddling a pony
On a home stretch.

Jokes about the weather,
The war, street car rush hours,
Women's white shoes
And wrist watches—
And sometimes:
Texas memories
Of Brann dying on a sidewalk in Waco,
Sending a death bullet into the heart
Of the one who gave Brann a death bullet—
And O. Henry searching life's corners and crimson
In the come and the go of life in Texas—
And O. Henry with iron wristlets on.

59

Isadora Duncan

She was a flame sheath of flesh made for dancing.
She believed she ran out into storm, rain, sun, and
became part of them and they were afterward woven
in her dances.

"The wind? I am the wind. The sea and the moon?
I am the sea and the moon. Tears, pain, love, bird-
flights? I am all of them. I dance what I am.
"Sin, prayer, faith the light that never was on land
or sea? I dance what I am."

Roses, lovers, money, children, came to her in her
life dance from California to Russia.
When her dancing days were not yet over but almost
come to an end, she died in a swift ride with a flame-red
scarf enwrapping her neck tighter and tighter. . . .

Sojourner Truth Speaking

I felt as if I had three hearts
and they were so large
my body could hardly hold them.

* *

If my cup won't hold but a pint
and yourn holds a quart,
wouldn't you be mean not to let me have
my little half-measure full?

* *

Here you are talking about being
"changed in the twinkling of an eye."
If the Lord should come
He'd change you to *nothing*
for there's nothing to you.

* *

Dat little man he say woman
can't have as much rights as man
'cause Christ wasn't a woman.
Whar did your Christ come from? Whar?
From God and a woman.
Man had nothing to do with Him.

* *

Jesus will walk with me through the fire
and keep me from harm.
Nothing belonging to God can burn,
any more than God himself.

61

I shall remain.
Do you tell me
that God's children
can't stand fire?

Mr. Lincoln and His Gloves

Mr. Lincoln on his way to Washington
to be the President of the United States
stays in New York City two days
and one night goes to the Opera.
Sits in a box, his lean speaking hands
      on a red velvet railing.
And the audience notices something.
Yes, notices.
Mr. Lincoln is wearing gloves
              kid gloves
              black kid gloves.

The style
the vogue
the fashion is white kid gloves.
On the main floor
in the balcony
in the boxes
the gloves are correct and white.

A gentleman in another box tells his ladies:
"I think we ought to send some flowers over the way
to the Undertaker of the Union."

Soon we see Mr. Lincoln in Washington kissing the Bible
swearing to be true to the Constitution.
Lincoln holding in his heart these words:
"I have not willingly planted a thorn in any man's bosom.
I shall do nothing through malice.
What I deal with is too vast for malice."

Now we see Mr. Lincoln at a White House reception
His fingers swollen, his white gloves
      twisted by a mob of handshakes.

His right hand at last giving an extra strong handshake
to an Illinois man, an Illinois man he knew long ago.
Then it happens!
His right glove cracks and goes to pieces.
He holds his hand up, looks at the dangling glove.
"Well, my old friend, this is a general bustification,
you and I were never meant to wear these things."

Another time, Mr. Lincoln rides away in a White House
    carriage.
Next to him an old western friend, wearing brand new
    white kid gloves.
Mr. Lincoln notices, can't help noticing those brand
    new white tight gloves.
Mr. Lincoln digs down into his pocket.
Feels around and brings out his own brand new white
    kid gloves,
begins squeezing his fingers and thumbs in
when the old friend cries:
"No, no, Mr. Lincoln,
put up your gloves, Mr. Lincoln."
And they ride along, talk and joke, no more bother,
                  sitting pretty
                  sitting easy
                  as two old worn gloves.

Often Mr. Lincoln cannot find his gloves.
Sometimes Mr. Lincoln forgets his gloves.
Often Mrs. Lincoln gives him a new pair, a nice, correct
fashionable pair of gloves.

And one day a California newspaper man
sees him hunting in his overcoat pocket
for a pair of gloves.
Bringing out one pair
he digs deeper
and brings out another pair.

Then into another pocket.
Out comes
            three
            four
            five
            six
            seven
            more pairs of gloves.

That was one time
if Mr. Lincoln had anything plenty of
it was gloves.

You and I may be sure Mr. Lincoln never in his life
felt sorry for himself about his gloves.

When he forgot his gloves
maybe he was too deep with remembering
men fighting, men dying, on consecrated ground.
Too deep with remembering
his hope
"Government of the people
by the people
for the people
shall not perish from the earth."

And there is no good reason why you,
                        why I,
                        why we
                        should ever worry
about Mr. Lincoln and his gloves.

Dune
Reflections

Pottawattamie Mask

The dirt of the earth gave me
to the things having me.
Where the dirt of the earth is
clean I am clean.
Where a stink comes from the earth
a stink comes from me.
Where the running waters run on
and never let up on their babble
babble babble, take a slant at me,
listen to my babble babble babble.

. .
. .

The big nose of an old Pottawattamie
bothered him by being heavy to carry
on the rampart of his face.
The big nostrils took in the breaths
of four blustering winds up and down
the Fox River hills in winter.
The big laughter of the old Pottawattamie
blustered out of the big nostrils meeting
the four winds half way.

. .
. .

Spread a long grin over your face.
Let the wind change while you hold the grin.
Then your face keeps that grin always.
The oldest Pottawattamies say this happens.

. .
. .

Hammer my head flat.
Square my shoulders to corners.
Flatten my curves from the armpits
    down to the big toe on each side.
Make me look the way you want me to look.
Whittle a cartoon of me, a wood cartoon from
    your knives; call it a wind god or a memory
    of a potato planter or one who looked at
    women and went away.

Cornshock in October

An illusion is a mouthful of air.
Blow it like a smoke ring, if you wish.
Watch the sag, the drift, the go-by of it.

Count your illusions, Oswald.
Count 'em like money is counted.
An illusion is better than a dollar bill
Or a couple of ten thousand dollar bills
On the days money buys nothing you want.

I saw a cornshock once in October.
It was an illusion of a cornshock—see?
It was a house with a thousand rooms.
I lived and died a thousand lives in it.
Six hundred windows swept a sea view,
Six or sixteen hundred, panels of blue silver
Set with struggling coal passers, oversea liners.
And another six hundred windows
(Or was it sixteen hundred?)
Took in mountains, took in prairies,
Panels of the struggling panoramas—
Yes, believe me, I lived and died there
A thousand lives, and for every life leaving me
I was reborn once.
     Now I am sitting in a November sun
     Sifting the warm corn gold in my fingers
And the one cornshock I knew in October
I count better than a dollar bill,
Better than a ten thousand dollar bill.

There was a shooting star.
I guess, Oswald, we'll call that an illusion too.
I picked it off the sky while it was falling.
I gave it the name of a priceless woman.

It fell, this shooting star, among the six hundred
Windows (or was it sixteen hundred)
Making panels of the coal passers and sea liners,
And the other six hundreds or sixteen hundreds
of windows, and the house of a thousand rooms
Arched and squared over the cornshock in October
Swept itself away leaving no epitaphs nor keepsakes,
Unless you say for me the face of a priceless woman,
Kept as a memory, is a keepsake.

And you'll say so?
Yes? An illusion is a mouthful of air?
I guess so. Blow 'em like smoke rings.

Poplars

A few poplars standing to the west
And one star and two stars and three,
And a sky changing ever so little
Yet changing, always changing
With playactors and lines and exits
On the stage of the west,
Cloud films coming, milky dust going,
And to this a few poplars singing, strumming,
Steady to the wind their music:
> This fills an evening hour.
> Here we loaf an hour, half a night.
> Here we find who keeps our memory.

White Wings

Sitting against a big friendly tree
> Reading a book I love,
> I looked up suddenly
And saw fleeting and wheeling
Away in the blue spring sky
> A flock of gray birds
Flashing white wings in the May sun.

Be Proud If You Want To

I watched tumble bugs one summer.
The tumble bugs respect each other.
I have seen one turn aside for another,
One bowing, "It is my luck to step out of the
      way for you."
If we were two tumble bugs we would both be funny.
Now I'm the only one of us that's funny.

Tell me you love me.
I want to hear that come from you.
Lie if you must, say it as half the truth.
Say it to play me along.
I'd rather you'd two-time me than throw me over.
Say it like something not to be meant.
Only tell it to me once: say you love me.

Be proud if you want to.
Be proud about your looks, the house you live in
And the high education your mother had
and the way she brought you up right.
You'll see there won't be a whimper out of me.
Be proud, but say it for me once.
Say it like a good actress.
Say you'd like to have me around.

Sun Music

Can a man carry in his head on a Sunday morning
memories with goat faces looking at him and calling?

There are the Hackensack marsh meadows
in a Saturday night sunset
of red sky pools
in a blur of red marsh pools.

There is a man's voice out of a shag hair
tumbling over a white forehead
talking about fifteen years
and the years fooled him
and brought him nothing.

There is a woman's voice out of a mouse-gray panel face
chiseled so-so, neither yes nor no, here nor there,
talking about fifteen years
and the years fooled her
and brought her nothing.

A white valley made up for it all.
A moon-white valley toward the Orange mountains
three o'clock in the September morning
and the houses slept on
and the people slept on
and only a line of yellow street lights
kept watch helping the moon
in some town across the river.

Chaminade's "Autumn" in the morning
made up for it all, a sun music getting
the wash on the early fire on the poplar leaves,
the deeper fire coming on the goldenrod and sumac,
and the phantom shine on falltime waters,
the twist and the mock on the Hackensack marshes.

On a Sunday morning
goat faces look at each other
in a man's head . .   and call . .

Hemstitches

April is near, the feel of the breath
of April is near, coming with a packsack
of whimsies.
(They tell me all winter April hides
and hemstitches—and now—now April
is going to pick loose the hemstitches.)
On the fields a low crying comes with
a low laughing—a bluebird goes on the
Kaw Valley and a redwing goes on the
Kaw Valley.
And a bluebird mate goes.
And a redwing mate goes.

Bumble Bee Days

The bumble bees clamber on the saw edges
            of gladiolas.
Lemon-rusty honey bees drone in the ears
            of hollyhocks.
Two leaves of a poplar drift among the
            watching asters.

Night Stars Over the Timberline

Kisses are cheap on a cool May night
When two lovers are lost on the timberline.
And the seven sisters dance and the dipper reels
And the show places of the sky
                            are a street of marching children.
Then . . the dry leaves mix with the new grass
And the knuckles of two hands tremble
To the earth's wireless repeating to far stars.
Then . . five words go for a thousand.
Bloodroot, trilliums and lady's slippers
Slip off their finger-rings
And swear to new sweethearts.

Horn Moon

The moon in the valley's end has two horns.
And there is a golden knob on the doors of the moon.
And they knock on the doors—whoever they are—
They knock all night and never get in.
There is a golden knob on the doors for luck
And there are two horns on the moon tonight
And I have a hat on a horn of the moon
And you have a hat on the horn of the moon
And the silver wimps are singing.

Alexander Flootenflirst Crosses the Monongahela River at Daybreak Lost in Meditation on Time Being Made of Moments

They come unbidden to smite me
so I stand unbidden smitten
   asking who smote me.
This is Alexander Flootenflirst speaking.
And I ask, sir, what are the facts,
For the facts come coiling to uncoil,
   to roll away as smoke rolls,
   to veer in spirals of illusion
   coiling back to facts again,
   events of revolving involvements,
   events fresh from the womb of time,
   events saying, "How do you do today?
   And how do you read my new face today?"
   till I have walked a room crying,
   "I don't know, my God, I don't know"
   till I have cooled myself in a calm pool
   and come out of it in a purple murmuring,
   "Time will tell, time and the night stars,
   Time and the births and deaths of time."
It may be well I know so much about nothing at all.
It may be well I know so little of everything everywhere.
For I know well I know little
And I know well how little is that little
I, Alexander Flootenflirst, asking, What, sir, are the facts?

   Now a practical man
a purchaser of potatoes for personal use
a partaker of onions for particular purposes
must beware of being smitten and asking who
   and whether a who or a what smote him.

So here
this mild person Alexander Flootenflirst
past midnight two-by-the-clock
and a pale half moon leans floats
at the shadowline of a naked skyscraper
    and the moon giving him a wink
    and the moon letting him know:
                    "Good going to you, sir."

Now the man takes the wink
and puts it in the thumb end
of his right hand glove
taking it as a coin to keep
a coin of personal sheen and shimmer
slide it under the brass bars
of a bank teller window
a voice of cool gunmetal comes:
"We don't seem to be acquainted, sir,
    with this species of currency."

And now the mild Alexander Flootenflirst
being accustomed to the bronx cheer,
to the razzberry, the brushoff, the bums rush,
we may see him now asking who or what smote him
and why early in the morning
before daylight beyond the Monongahela River
in a light ravel of moon mist
amid baby bundles of fluff white
five little stars bunch themselves
and stand forth as a blossom of rose flame
while yet he keeps in a glove thumb end
the moon coin given earlier, the moon wink,
the high respect of the moon for him,
the fond and fleeting wish of the half moon:
                    "Good going to you, sir."

Then it smites Alexander Flootenflirst
and he stands smitten with the wonder
of time being made of moments
and you can fold one and lay it cold
with the ashes of other forgotten moments
while another gets locked and held
to go burning itself deeper ever
in the memento flame line of a rose blossom
or a moon coin in a glove thumb end.

    Yet a practical man must beware.
A purchaser of potatoes, a partaker of onions
must seize on the contradictions involved
in a bus driver telling fares to Punxsutawney:
"Take   your   time, steplivelyplease,
       take   your   time, steplivelyplease."

    His mind wanders—
well knows Alexander Flootenflirst
    his mind wanders
    till he picks his target
    and shrinks it
    to a bubble of nothing
    with his mighty meditations:—

The steel of a tall lean skyscraper stands as fact
    or illusion: you suppose whatever you like.
You can suppose it stands there ever and always in
    a late afternoon slide of prisms to a sunset bath
    and an evening dusk of checkered lights.
You can suppose the swelling total volume of business
    done behind those windows will break all previous
    records this year and come along next year with an-
    other smashing rise of sales volume.
You can suppose on floor over floor the sales force and
    the production end divide into moon shooters and those
    holding it is not good policy to shoot at the moon.

Or you can suppose the skyscraper swaying ever so slightly
    in the wind of a dusk before dawn telling the moon:
"One of these years the moon shooters will tear me down for
    scrap and put up what they like better to look at."

He walks talking and talks walking and midway over a bridge
    sees himself both a who and a what, fact and illusion, an
    etching, a painting, a photograph mural, titled:
"Alexander Flootenflirst Crosses the Monongahela River at Day-
    break Lost in Meditation on Time Being Made of Moments,"
Knowing well this exterior view gives nothing of a flame-line
    blossom nor a moon coin in a glove thumb end nor the high
    respect of the moon for him, the fond and fleeting wish:
                                "Good going to you, sir."

Buns and Gardenias

On Avenue A or B I read a sign:
Manhattan Ashcan Manufacturing Company.
In one of the suburbs I passed another:
whizzing past I got it on the fly:
Sensitive Research Instrument Corporation.

And I knew I had a vested interest in each.
I am an ashcan. I am a sensitive instrument.
((If this bothers you for a moment please go
    immerse your excellent head elsewhere and
    leave me in my own tubs of folly.))
I am an ashcan. I am a sensitive instrument.

Often and often hot buns on a plate
are good as fresh gardenias in a bowl.
In case of doubt take the hot buns
and afterward look long at the flowers.
The game goes back a long time and is also
played with rye bread and red roses,
        with hyacinths and biscuits.

Yah you too are an ashcan,
        you too a sensitive instrument.
Maybe you see yourself here five sacraments of dust.
Maybe moonwhite and pale gold you see yourself here.

Floodlights

From the Michigan Avenue River Bridge Chicago 1931

Floodlights send a steady tinting
on the tall skyscraper.
Munificent quiet hours pass while
a dominant sentinel watches.
The traffic cops, the night patrols,
they too watch.
Out on the waters, over the land, are
many watchers.
They take special notice of the arcs
and shadows.
They tell each other how the floodlights
operate.
The architect put up the walls with the
idea of floodlights.
The mention of how beautiful it is may
be discussed.
As a proud accomplishment of man's genius
it may be discussed, and
As the last word in man's cunning of high
construction.
The men selling apples, lead pencils,
in the dusk—
The professional panhandlers or those who
rake in the garbage dumps—
The faded silhouettes technically classified
as the technologically disemployed—
Also the unemployed, the unemployable, who daylong
deploy murmuring job ahoy job ahoy—
These too, their wives, daughters, kith, kin, kisses,
if any, may be discussed.
The mention of how they get by or how they die
day by day can be taken up.
The smooth broadcasters at the mikes among the
floodlights—

They can tell the world humanity is both
beautiful and tragic.
    The hoom h o o m of a big steamboat
    ready to dock—
    This mixes in the air and rises high
    into the floodlights—
    Into the spikes and waves laid white
    and gleaming—
    On the steel and concrete sentinel
    standing almost dumb—
    Standing with the almost frozen query,
    Why am I here? why am I here?

Franciscan

Have you sat with poverty and tried
to guess its dirty riddles?
Then maybe we can travel together.
Have you torn off pages of struggle
too mean to remember—and looked at a
long scar as a sphinx?
Then we might find a lingo
for signals.
Have you lived alone in a house with
rats gnawing, gnawing, in the few quiet
hours?
Then maybe we can talk about things.
Have you written letters and dropped
them in a fire saying: "Nobody home—
what's the use?
Then we can pass the time a little while.
Have you met scarecrows and mumbled, "Why!
I know *you* and *you* and *you*"?
Then we can look at each other's faces.
Have you sat with the deaf, the dumb, the
blind, the broken, saying, "I belong! I belong!"?
Then we can touch fingertips and sit
for a quiet hour.
Have you gone deep in a dusty turmoil till
the street corners whirled and you forgot
your name and number?
Then we can laugh together over what
we lost and found.

Bribery

Longer ago than any living man remembers
as long ago as John Ball or Wat Tyler
the bribe was a scrap of bread
given by a good Christian to a beggar.
The giver was proud to be seen bribing.
The beggar, the taker, received the bribe
in broad daylight, thankful to be bribed.
    Now in the winding convolutions of speech,
    and the inscrutable transmutations of time,
    the giver of a bribe and the taker of a bribe
    hide themselves from any and all witnesses,
each understanding, "this is on the Q.T.—
this is a secret not even wild horses
               could drag from me."

There are ways and ways.
The giver of the bribe may put it in a box
    telling the taker where to find the box,
    neither seeing the face of the other
    when the taker gets his fingers on the bribe.

Or the bribe giver may stand before the taker
and say with a face of bland innocence,
"I brought you something—it's in my left coat pocket."
The taker too wears a face of bland innocence.
They stand before each other in a mutual innocence.

Or the giver may find the taker has a debt
he is losing sleep over,
looks into his compassionate heart and
brings himself to ask the taker
if he may pay this debt
               so there may be no more lost sleep.

This has the color of a Christian act,
a likeness to giving a beggar a scrap of bread,
thus within the earliest meaning of "bribery."
Yet required it is and the pledge clear:
   on the giver being asked he shall not say,
                      "Yes, I paid the man's debt,"
   nor shall the taker answer, "Yes, he paid my debt."
Good men and excellent lawyers have gone through this
   ordeal and called it not so much of an ordeal after all.

           I can't give it to you exactly, brother.
           I have it on a piece of paper
                 where I wrote it years ago.
           I can give you the gist of it, though,
                 as from President Charles Eliot of Harvard:
                    "The greatest danger
                        of the American republic
                    is
                        secret influence."
"Why should you be troubled
     or anybody be troubled
        about the American republic?"
You can hear that question with a horselaugh
from givers and takers and their wives
        saying, "We like nice things,"
or, "Sure, we're for the American republic
     and what you don't know won't hurt you."

           Longer ago than any living man remembers
           the bribe was a scrap of bread
           given by a good Christian to a beggar,
           in broad daylight
           before two, ten, or sixty witnesses—

Studies in Green Blinds

The green blinds of old Indiana houses,
Oblong panels of Indiana grass thoughts,
Tell their story on white houses,
Sun thoughts level white on old Indiana houses.
The green blinds of old Ohio houses,
Tell their story on red brick walls.
It is grass and sun over again.

Cages

In the zoo are iron cages where steel bars keep lions and
      wolves, tigers and bearcats, away from us.
Downtown in the banks and stores are more cages where steel
      bars keep us away from cashiers and money-counters.
There is a distinction here between being outside looking in
      and inside looking out.

High Class Bums

Be a high class bum, if you can;
     other people work for you.
Nothing to do till tomorrow; then
     it's all done for you by those thankful to
     get jobs from you.
All you do is eat, sleep, tell the chauffeur, the
     butler, the valet, the cook, when and what; ride,
     shoot, gamble, play polo, fly, yacht, meet with the
     trustees and the other directors or chase any
     little international chippy you choose; marry
     first one, then another, till you have had eight
     wives; it's a life; you go to Paris, Monte Carlo,
     the South Seas, China, Africa, or the moon; or
     you can shoot yourself or step out of a ten-story
     window and let 'em pick up the corpus delicti in
     black silk pajamas; it's been done.
The men in the mines and mills, the bozos butting
     through blizzards with extra fare trains, the lads
     on the assembly line, they'll read about you; the
     kids'll see you on TV, in the tabloids, in the
     newsreels and say, "That's him."
Be a high class bum, if you can.

Each Its Own World

Trumpet vine blossoms climb and spill
with seven fingers unfolding one by one
seven flowers of tawny brown crimson,
unfailing black stripes of velvet
        hidden cool and measured inside.

We can be sentimental about them or practical
as humming-birds: they flutter in wing whirr
the torso held to a standstill, the beak plunging
to the food it sucks from the blossom.

Large black ants of endless determinations,
Small blue ants minding every passing moment,
Eager to make use of the fractions of time,
Gray spiders with yellow belly bands and stripes
—into the blossoms they go and scurry,
seekers, hustlers for the day's eating.

Moonsheen

Beware of the moonsheen when the moon
is tipsy under the wind.
The Irish, the Persians, the Senegambians,
have read that terror and told of it
in tall books.
Much more might be spoken of the moon,
my lady, my looloo, my only one.
The moon keeps many wedding dresses;
the shouting of the shivaree boys is ready;
the rice, confetti, old shoes, nickering, and
the legends pasted on luggage: just married.
To the gamblers the moonsheen gives hunches;
the unwashed sock to be buried at midnight
must have a moonsheen fall on it or you will
be racked with rheumatism; those crazy over
horses are loony with a moonsheen spell; the
moon buys joybells maybe.
Be careful how you think too often of this
bauble, the moon, my lady, my looloo, my only one.

You Have Chosen

Leaves in the wind, you have chosen
to fly.
Rocks in the river, you have chosen
to stand.
But wind and water who told you to
roam and run?

Florence Ayscough Translates a Chinese Poem

The cold rain connects the sky and river.
Night enters Wu.
At dawn my friend will depart alone for
　　Mount Tsu.
When arrived at Lo Yang he will write to
　　those dear to me
That my heart is as a piece of ice in a
　　bowl of jade.

Whangpoo Bittersweet

Somewhere in the years plowed under and gone
to the tombs of the Mings and the Hongs,
to the last of the Tings and their Tong wars,
before the Japs buckled with the heat of empire,
before the British broke their paths in China,
before Standard Oil brought kerosene in cans
to the lamps of Woohoo huts—and boats of Bibles
moved up the bends of the Whangpoo seeking
the children of Confucius to teach them—
long before these tasted bittersweet—
and earlier in time than our friend Li Po
who laughed and drank over his poems
he found so often either too bitter, too sweet,
winning seldom into a bittersweet gathered
of wry earth and white windflower, sea wrack
and blue mist: he got it a few times.

    Li Po you may have heard
    (they still tell about it
    in Woo Hoo and along the Whangpoo)
    picked a moment for an exit,
riding a river barge and seeing a golden plate,
a shining moon alive and singing on the waters
    giving him an idea for a poem
so he dives headfirst off the brass rail
into the float of the baffling moongold pool
making it his own forever and ever
keeping his moon secrets in his own drenched hands,
holding forever his personal chosen bittersweet.

    One grandfather of Li Po told him how
    farther back than anyone could remember
    they were saying along the Whangpoo an old poem,
    a smooth dark poem only slightly tarnished:

you could see them buy and sell it back and forth,
the price asked being a little less than
nothing at all, take it or leave it,
and no one could think about it and haggle:

> Draw sword: cut water:
> water still flow.

> Lift cup: drown sorrow:
> sorrow still sorry.

Effects in Hard Metal

Let me ask again for a brass love.
I am tired of heart shapes in gold.
I am done with yesterdays made into gold wishes.

The precious porcelain dish
Once had blessings spoken over it.
Now it is knocked by a laughing evil elbow
To the level tile floor,
Forty pieces for forty junk wagons.

Now I ask a dented copper bowl for my oatmeal, my soup.
Twice a year we will take pumice stone and a rag
And sit in the sun and polish the copper bowl.

The glint of copper under an apple tree in summer
Is a moonshaft left over from night time.

Who Knows?

Russet shadows circle the navel of a tree.
Seventeen hokku syllables might gather it.
Does not a city of ants reduce its endless zigzag
Confusions to one design?
The russet of the shadows comes from color kilns of the sky,
Of the navel of the sun.

The lips of a red flower win their crimson by night.
The carriers of carnation tints step softly.
The bringing of color to a scarlet runner is by a silent sifting.
Interfusions such as these are a whisper wisdom; they vanish
                    mentioned aloud.
As to soft loves and loud the loud ones never last.

What does "ashes of love" mean?
It is a phrase for a fire gone out.
What does "triumphant love" mean?
It is an abstract noun and a modifying adjective.
Is there no half-way point between these two?
Yes, at all hours, in all months, in huts and mansions.
Who knows when love fails,
When love wins?
Little watchers; they will
Sing or they won't; they leave
Keepsakes or they don't.

Let Winter Come

Let winter come; these days have too many
living leaves; the speech of the sun
and these leaves is too much; the yellow
of the yellow asters, the purple of the
purple asters, the white ghost mushrooms
wearing pink and cream grey sheath gowns,
they are too much; let winter come.

Let winds come killing all flowers; let the
summer songs die; the winds are too warm too
many long months; the slide of a bird warbler's
cry in the night, the branches hanging with
leaf patterns at the summer sky, are too near,
too near; let the gray winter come.

           . .
           . .

It was the same southwest wind again
crossing the yellow aster leaves,
in the morning eyes of the brown-eyed Susans,
in the toadflax sheaves, smiling butter-and-eggs,
in the white mushrooms sprung from air into air;
it was the same southwest wind.

It is this wind keeps our airy keepsakes,
keeps our lost pages of notes scribbled
on how the days go by, how our talk runs away
on the wind, how the running wind means well,
how the field people, asters, toadflax, mushrooms,
      rise, sing, go away,
      leaving in the air
      no last testament at all,
leaving no message at all on how this sister,
that brother, those cousins, such and such sweethearts

are remembered with a gold leaf, a rainbow,
a shimmer of one haunted moonray who came as a chattel
to be kept and passed on in a last testament—
here no scribblings at all only those put on our lost pages,
our keepsakes of loam and loam talk across a summer, a spring;
it is this wind keeps our airy keepsakes.

"Good-by, my doors and windows," said a child I love,
and this child is a gypsy cousin of the spring wind
coming from the spring sky with many doors and windows
to open—and time to open them—
by night with a moon and shadow plays,
by day with a sun and shadow plays—and time to open them—
a wet wing murmur and a leap and a leap over of curves—
and time to open them—this is the wind, our wind,
the keeper of our airy keepsakes.

The Trees Wait

In April, early April,
The trees wait.

Little in the air to be seen,
Only rain and sun after rain
Till a tremblegreen comes.

In October, late October,
The trees wait.

The sky hears—
What doesn't the sky hear
of the wind and the leaves
talking?

                The trees wait.

Free Winds

Winds among the treetops
     dance on the bellies of the trees and they
     shake out the hair of the trees and tease the
     high limbs with a grand whining.

They take violins some nights and accordions and
     scrape off tall music and blow out tall music
     and they pull out stops and handle roaming
     chords gladder than farm-hands Saturday nights.

Early in the Morning

The silk silversheet of the spider cobwebs
early, early in the morning and the sun,
I must name these and those
if you ask me how and when,
if you ask me who and where
there are people hard to forget—
The spinning sheets of the silver spiders,
early, early before the winds and the wheels
    begin—early, early before the horses and
    the horns—before the snaffles of the wagons
    begin working—
early then I name these and those, I count the
    money of my memories.

Being Born Is Important

Being born is important.
You who have stood at the bedposts
and seen a mother on her high harvest day,
the day of the most golden of harvest moons for her.

You who have seen the new wet child
dried behind the ears,
swaddled in soft fresh garments,
pursing its lips and sending a groping mouth
toward the nipples where white milk is ready—

You who have seen this love's payday
of wild toil and sweet agonizing—

You know being born is important.
You know nothing else was ever so important to you.
You understand the payday of love is so old,
So involved, so traced with circles of the moon,
So cunning with the secrets of the salts of the blood—
It must be older than the moon, older than salt.

. .   . .

Leavetaking

Kiss me for luck once.
Kiss me for a memory too.
Kiss me quick only to be kissing.
    I will be gone long.
    Polar bears are kind
    yet the icy winds eat;
    claws of arctic frost,
    they too eat, and loneliness,
    worst of all, eats.

    Kiss me three times,
        for luck,
        for memory,
And quick, once, only to be kissing.

Mister Altgeld

The authority of the law comes with a club and a gun
With a star and a shield, bracelets and a warrant.
Then comes the conflict of the majesty of the law
With the majesty of the individual, the citizen, the person.
Sometimes one wins, sometimes another.
The result is always either silence submission yes yes
Or no no history shibboleths banners memorials
Bronze statues in public parks where sparrows
And purple martins sharpen their bills
On the bronze elbows amid the verdigris
Of the enshrined figure of a hero.

Walls of Rooms

Walls of rooms are young and old, sad and gay.
They change as the faces of people change.

The wall north of my typewriter
Says Lincoln sat in a tent with McClellan.
The president folds his hands
And listens across the war maps
To the warrior who lost one campaign and another.

The wall tells what Rembrandt thought
of an old woman cutting her finger nails.

Grant in '64 at City Point.
The general crosses his legs.
He doesn't care for looks.

The American aviators in France, Maximilian Harden,
Woodrow Wilson, a battleship in a hurricane,
A crew of plugmen and sight-setters, shirts off,
Working a 7-inch gun.

A war map of Europe.
Drenched fields from Mesopotamia to London.
Tumults from Madrid to Archangel.

Walls of rooms are young and old, sad and gay.
They change as the faces of people change.

Let the Years Go Softly Enough
To Edwin Ford Piper

Let the years go softly enough
and I will yet make the canoe trip
you gesture about, casually with your
        thumb, standing on the river bridge
        over the Iowa river at Iowa City.

Below the bridge the falls murmured
and the black even sheet of water
between the bridgeway and the falls
crossed itself with two green streaks
        of lamplights.

It was there you jerked your thumb
toward the falls and told me you let
your canoe down there and followed the
        river and never met another waterfall
        and you and your canoe ended on the
        Mississippi near Keokuk.

And you had been speaking of the old cannon
        on the campus and how old Ossawatomie Brown
        bought that cannon mumbling his gaunt hopes
        of human freedom and Christ and sinners.

Let the years go softly enough and you and I
        will understand Old Ossawatomie and his old
        cannon and his mumblings.
Let the years go softly enough and you and I may
        take that canoe trip from below the falls and
        on among the curves that end on the Mississippi
        near Keokuk.
Let the years go softly enough and we may stand again
        watching where the falls murmur and the black even
        sheet of water crosses itself with two streaks of
        green light.

108

Young Brother

No not now not yet
and you see no dream
worth dying for
not yet it is too early.

And the wind may come blowing
till in its crazy roar one day
it takes two men to hold
           one man's hair on.

In that time and that weather
eat the shame and dirt
of each yes-yes you say
or you choose between two dreams
and for each men are dying
and the proof of the dream
comes after comes later
and is named History:
the makers of this called History
are the fools of dream and death:
they say what happens
and afterward their say-so
as to what did happen
is the one story: no other stands.

You will be there my young brother
cool in the smoke and wrath
if in our time that wild weather comes
        and it takes two men to hold
        one man's hair on.

                1932

Two Commentaries on Humpty Dumpty

Humpty Dumpty was nobody's fool
Even though it is a classic tale
How he knew nothing to begin with,
Learned nothing, came to nothing.—
An egg, sitting on a wall, they tell it.—
And he took a tumble and they could never
Put the pieces of him together again.

Whether he was a good egg or a bad egg,
Whether he was inspected, approved, passed,
Whether he was scrub or thoroughbred,
The record says nobody knows
And if they did they wouldn't tell.

Whether he climbed up the wall by himself,
Whether somebody else put him up on the wall,
Whether he was pushed off, shoved without
Anybody asking him, "Are you ready to go?"—
Whether he said, "I've been an egg long enough,
And it's time for me to take a tumble"—
Whether it was just an accident and other eggs
Looking on said, "He was a good egg and we're sorry,"
Or, "He was a bad egg and it's just as well"—
Whether this or that happened and *why*
The recorders of Humpty have not told us.
He fell off a wall and that was the end.
Your guess is as good as the next one on the why of it.

He may never have sat on a wall before.
He may have been lifted onto the wall by other eggs
Laughing, "We shall give this egg a great fame."
He looked from the wall to the gravel far down.
He became dizzy thinking how high up he was
And the high cost of having fame, of listening

To the murmur far below of many little eggs
Repeating, "We shall give this egg a great fame."
From being dizzy he changed to being lonely.
He kept saying, "Jesus, it's cold up here,
Why was I lifted up here to be alone
And no other egg for me to say to 'how cold,
How far, how lonely, it is up here'?"
He either fell off because he wanted to,
Dropping down headfirst calling, "Here goes!"
Or he was dizzy, cold, lonely, and found himself
Falling before he could do anything about it.

         . .   . .   . .

Many crops came to their harvest time,
Many oxen and mules struggled in the fields.
The long wars and the short wars came
Each with its red spill of boys dying.
Many sands ran through the glass of time
And old clocks ran down, wore out, had their places
Taken by new clocks in turn wearing out, running down.
Iron oxen and mules of steel arrived on the earth.
And they turned rust and ran down like the clocks
And had their places taken by always better models.
Into the arch of sky man launched himself as an eagle
And a droning burden-bearer and a laugher at distance
Hugging the earth only when he had to,
Dropping to the gravel when there was nothing else to do.
And man the flyer, like man the mule driver, had his story
Of an old timer, Humpty Dumpty, dizzy, cold, lonely.
Dropping down headfirst calling, "Here goes!"
Or falling before he could do anything about it.
         Yes: Humpty Dumpty was nobody's fool.

Amberdamber
After reading Nietzsche

"What have you in your head?" they asked Amberdamber.
And he answered, "Categories, hierarchies, axioms, queries."
They said, "Give us a few of the queries, only a few."
He spoke, "Why do some babies have dimples and others none?"
And again, "When Nebuchadnezzar had to eat grass did he learn
                                                    to like it?"
Or, "Did Monkey Face Charley have a monkey face or was it just
                                            a nickname?"
Or, "When you write on white paper with white ink what does it say
                            and who can read it?"
They said, "Now tell us about your categories, hierarchies,
                                                axioms."
He said, "Today is my day for queries, tomorrow and day by day I
            will give you my tumultuous categories, my farflung
            hierarchies, and my shimmering glittering cascading
            axioms."
                        Thus spake Amberdamber
                        and they heard him gladly
                        and they respected him
                        and they tried to imitate him.

Jones

It wasn't so easy, what with
a job he had to hold so as to eat,
what with girls he met who had tricks,
and a little woman he took up with
who was willing to marry a Jones,
what with bills to pay, rent, clothes,
groceries, movies, radio, a car, doctors.
" 'Tain't so easy as you might think,"
was the way Jones told it.

Then Jones died.
Ten millions like him
died for God and country
and slept in garments of dust.
They lay beyond all tumults.

Horses hauling great guns went trampling
over the odd little corner of the earth
where Jones lay swaddled in his last ashes.
The guns snarled, roared and boomed.
And Jones slept on.
The night guns sent shells screaming
with intentions to kill off the living
and make the dead sit up and say something.
But Jones slept on.
The earth was torn and plowed by shells.
An iron can of dynamite dug in and
uprooted Jones. He lay on his face.
But he refused to sit up.
He refused to speak.
He lay in a dusty garment beyond all tumults.
He had arrived at majesty.
He had gone to the great house of many people
where men forget and are friends again.

Nearer Than Any Mother's Heart Wishes

1

In the month of February Eighteen Sixty One
there was a saint in Charleston, South Carolina
and everybody loved him for what he had of
humor, patience, understanding, compassion:
he was soft and hard and nobody's fool,
standing over six feet, heavy jowls, big mouth,
swarthy skin, oily black hair straight
down the slope of his broad back.
   And he sees war coming North and South.
He meets a man one morning asking him which way
to the Lunatic Asylum—and James Louis Petigru
answers by pointing north, south, east, west:
   "Go any way at all—you can't go wrong—
   The whole country has gone crazy!"

2

After Ghengis Khan had burned a thousand barns,
wrecked a hundred towns, and killed and killed
more people than he had time to count
he heard an old peasant woman say one day:
"Now this here Ghengis Khan where did he come
   from? I never heard of him."
And it changed his ideas about name and fame.

3

After Napoleon had crossed one country
and let them know who he was
people looked at what was left
of the homes and crops, saying:
"Next year the roses will be more blood-red.
It was like that after the last war."

And yet Napoleon—what did he know about war?
And does he look like an amateur today?
Did he ever see motorized units whirling
Over hard roads with troop replacements?
Or tanks giving cavalry the horselaugh?
Or a roving skyrider with a load of TNT?
Or an undersea boat releasing a torpedo?
Or a machine gun brigade landing from parachutes?
Or a rolling yellow wall of mustard gas
guaranteed to make them cry and mow them down?
Or civilian populations drilled for air raids?
Napoleon yes he could come back and take lessons.
And Sherman, old William Tecumseh, he too could come
back and say, "War is hell and stinks worse than ever."

4
Think about anything cold now
for the sake of keeping cool.
    Be a piece of ice.
Think about yourself as a long icicle.
Think about the winter northern lights,
shivering splinters of the aurora borealis.
Consider the Arctics: tell yourself a story
about someone just a little coo-coo
climbing the North Pole for the view
        wearing an ice hat
        where the nights are six months long.

5
Advice is cheap: in one ear and out the other.
And you can hear anything you want to hear.
And this is a free country and you can walk
right up to any other man and say:
"Excuse me while I give you an earful."

And furthermore this being a free country
he can tell you when you are through:
"Where have I heard that chatter before?"
This happens every day in a time when
garrulous man never before had so many things
whereby to be garrulous:
billboards by day, neon signs by night,
telegraph, telephone, teletype, ticker tape,
phonograph recordings, electrical transcriptions,
extra extry uxtra newspaper mister the latest,
sound films, sound trucks, newsreels,
amplifiers, public address systems, loud speakers,
skywriting airplanes mentioning dog food,
undersea cables and transoceanic phone and wireless,
high fidelity transmitters of your slightest word,
your cough or your whisper in the little mike
going coast to coast and to other continents.

And the head of man, the noggin, the bean,
the reservoir located above the ears,
the top floor seething, swarming, alive,
the little garret sometimes half empty
and only a few crippled bats flying—
into these rooms of the human brain they launch
their loads of propaganda and call it good—
torpedoes of hate germs, plasms of passion—
unimpeachable giant facts glibly twisted into
shuddering fantasies of dripping maniac dwarfs—
honest questions of common men answered with lies—
unanswerable questions given slimy adroit answers—
stuffed prophets strutting their stuff—
minor mouthpieces imitating the majors—
one Manhattan bureau of public relations saying:
"We can make the people believe anything we want
    them to."

Nevertheless one Sunday morning leaving St. Joe, Missouri
a brakeman, a stinger, walks into the smoker
and flops himself alongside a fireman in overalls,
alongside a tallowpot bothering nobody, asking with a grin,
    "What do you know today for sure?"
And the answer came with a grin and a slow finality:
    "Not a damn thing."

The innocent bystander is not always so innocent
as he looks: he can tell a hawk from a handsaw
and is ready to swear on a stack of Bibles that
a horse chestnut and a chestnut horse are never
the same: he may ask "Is that so?" and if you
prove it then ask "What of it?" having notions
of his own: he is careless slinging grammar around
knowing "Some of 'em that ain't sayin' ain't ain't eatin'."

6
There are ideas tied up with dreams.
Too often these dreams are wild and crazy.
They get going in the blood of men.
    Then history begins popping.
    Then hell breaks loose.
    Fast or slow the hell spends itself.
Then everybody takes a rest and wonders
when and where hell will break loose next.
This is the chart of the fever and curse
of pre-war, war, post-war, and again later
pre-war, war, post-war.

7
Any mother might be hearing her boy child now asking:
"Mama what is this supreme sacrifice I hear about?"
And answering, "Supreme sacrifice is when you go to
    war and die for your country."

117

Any mother might be saying now:
"The cool music of deep hearts is on me.
The fathoms of ancient fears are on me."

Nearer than any mother's heart wishes
now is heartbreak time.

8
Be steady now and keep your shirt on
like George Washington did when
he heard the crying out loud in his time—
would that be good advice?

Be cool as death now
Like Old Abe Lincoln kept cool
when a hurricane began snarling—
would that be good advice?

Try to figure it out for yourself
remembering figures can lie
and liars can figure
and some promises are not worth
the paper they are written on.

They are changing the maps
of Europe, Asia, and Africa—
they are changing the maps like always.

Over pieces of land they are wrangling,
over iron and oil and fat lands,
over breed and kin and race pride,
over poisons, balloons, baboon reachings—
    and the little wars are leading on
    into the big war to come.

Who could have given us the lowdown
on why Mussolini
poured troops and planes into Spain?

Who explained why Hitler
threw heavy guns and flying bombers
to the help of Franco
and the Mohammedan Moors of France
and the cause of Liberty and God in Spain
and the iron works
and the mineral deposits of Spain?
How will his slogans die
and his abracadabra vanish?

9
Be steady now and keep your shirt on.
    Be cool as death if you can.
Try to figure it out for yourself.

    Behind this awful music
is a more awful music to come?
They are changing the maps like always.

    Study the make of a gas mask
    how to wear it over your face
    how to conduct yourself wearing it
in rooms and streets, in your daily doings.

    They gaze as silent baboons
    in the guise of long snouts
though under this outer guise they are
human wanderers with nostrils seeking
    air, oxygen, freedom, peace.

Under the fantasies of these skulls
runs the hope of human dignity
                    somehow, sometime.

10
    Presents are delivered from the sky,
    in every package a prize, a chance,
    to choke, to suffocate, to forget
yes to forget every last word ever spoken of
man higher in the scale than animal creation,
the gorilla and the tiger being mere beasts
while man has shrines, altars, lights,
books awarding him personal immortality,
    books not yet banned nor burned.

    Let yourself be
    imperturbable as brass candlesticks
    or ancient folios bound in leather
    holding common prayers on parchment
    with the calm of an ivory crucifix when
shattered glass showers the chairs, the floor, the desk,
splinters and dust of glass cover the bath-tub bottom,
when plaster drops on the breakfast cloth
not long before the walls hesitate and totter
and the roof caves in (as in Hangkow or Canton),
when (as in Madrid) the sirens sound and the ambulances
pick up in the streets the mutilated still breathing
and carry them to hospitals not yet bombed and wrecked.

    Few of us will take it
    and say it is good
    The old wars were
    something else again.
Now babies will have baby-size gas masks.

120

The time to be hard and bitter
    —is that time now?
Or shall we insist on asking now the
    ancient question:
"What do the people get for the wars
    they fight with each other?

11

    The human heart weaves consolations.
    And they are made of what?
Of thin air—of the blue substance of the
    shadows of bones—
of a stuff so finespun it has the the heft of mist,
    merely mist
or the desperate balance between discipline and
    freedom.

    Men fight for dreams of freedom
    finding later they fought for
    land, for trade routes, for empire,
    for markets and controls,
    for gains in cash and dominance.

Yet again men fight for dreams of freedom
and win footholds for human rights,
measurable gains for mankind:
in the strife of strikes and wars
                    sometimes this happens
                    as a poem of action
                    long remembered.

12

Now in the looking glass of our time
now we have seen rehearsals for what?

The grinning cats of accomplished fact
    sit wiping their faces.
Thus it was in Shanghai, in Bilbao, in Ethiopia,
    in Vienna on the blue Danube.

    The story keeps going:
    a serial to be concluded
sometime in the rolling of the ivories,
    in the shuffling of cards,
in the heads-or-tails of circumstance,
    sometime.

    Some had names and numbers.
    They are rubbed out.
To them came the bloody trucks
    and the published orders
    and the secret arrests
    and the public atrocities
    and the studied punishments
    of concentration camps.

    Day by day they march—
    the living dead men
    remembering dimly how
    they had freedom:
"and the next day it rained."

13
    The crying of red flowers
    is to come in the sky.
Farther yet the revolving blossoms
    of the bombing squadrons.

    Spain shall spread.
    China shall not be alone.

Neither Addis Ababa nor liberty
is a final and willing corpse.

Too many corpses refused to be
final and willing corpses.
They talk now in their last sleep:
    and they are heard:
    these losers are heard.

The earth may yet seem covered with losers.
Nevertheless before the last platoon of losers is shot,
Before the last corpse gets a storm-trooper kick in the face
There will be fresh foreshadowings on the air.
    For the winners never win in this game
    and keep their winnings: it is so written.
    Corpses can be flung in a hole:
                        shadows march on.

The losers so often come back
ghosting their conquerors.
    There are not nails enough
    to nail down victory.
No more can absolute conquest be kept without change
than you can take wool and weave garments for shadows.

Spain yes, China yes, Austria ja:
they are beginnings:
yet to come is the drama and its Act I,
    Act II, Act III—and so on.

Their lost men took a hand so often
in items of sheer valor, no music nor flowers,
dying without witnesses nor loved ones at hand
    nor enough fragments
    to put in a basket for burial.

You young ones, you darlings of destiny,
before your eyes too
shall unfold the sheets of fire and the call:
      popular fronts and governments
      shall not perish from the earth:
      is this the word? this from
      that shovel of dust and valor in Spain—
even though a fraction of them had only a notion
to take a whirl at the wild game of war
and flirt with death for the fun of it?

The timing of their laughter
may be mentioned—
those who spat in the dust
saying, "What the hell? Who wants
      to live forever anyhow?"

14
      One may speak as no prophet at all,
      as a traveler taking it slow
      over a mug of java with ham on rye,
as a citizen troubled over storm warnings,
over black roses, heavy roses in the sky,
and heavy heavy heavy hangs over thy head.

      They are changing the maps
      of Europe, Asia, Africa,
they are changing the maps like always.
Be steady now and keep your shirt on.
      Be cool as death if you can.
Try to figure it out for yourself.

The lilacs of April are good to look at.
So are the oaks of gold in the fall of the year

And the whirl of snow in the winter time
      and the growing corn in summer.
They carry beautiful fables
      for those having time to look and see.

And yet—what of it? who cares?
When young men arc cut down like cornstalks
and cathedrals go down like oaks under lightning
and lilacs wither from the breath of gas—
                what of it? who cares?

    When shall men be hard and bitter,
    open and public and incessant
    in the asking of that terrible question:
"What do the people get for the wars they fight
                with each other?"

Any mother might be saying now:
"The cool music of deep hearts is on me.
The fathoms of ancient fears are on me."

Nearer than any mother's heart wishes
now is heartbreak time.

                        1938

Mountain
Echoes

Remembers

There is the way the wind blows
when the wind blows all day, all night,
blowing always the same name, the same face—
or the snow when the snow falls all day, all night.
snowing the same white name, the same white face,
the snow, the wind, coming always with remembers.

There is the way the sea and the moon remember
piling the white horses over and under
rocks and shingles, shoreline and sand.
washing and tumbling in foam and light—
every white horse one of your remembers,
the water, the moonfall, holding your remembers.

There is the way the rain comes down
when the rain comes down all day, all night,
the same blue rain, gray rain, purple rain,
slow rain coming down in your bones and blood,
in the bones of your head, the blood of your heart,
raining the same name, the same face always—
        what is it?   what do you call it?

The day fades and becomes the night
and the night fades and becomes the day
fading the same name again, the same face,
finding a fine smoke over the night stars
and moving away the smoke in two white whispers
of one remember, two remembers, many many more—
        what is it?   remembering?   only remembering?

In street or road or room where you go,
big open rooms with long glass chandeliers,
little shut rooms with lighted candles,
sunny corners with small square clocks

counting the seconds, chiming the hours with bells
and one face, one name, circle your head and bones
and your remembers wash you, blow you, hold you
     in the wind, the sea, the moon,
     in the rain, the night, the smoke stars,
     in the rooms, the clocks, the bells.

Seven Impressions

Passion is a flower.
So they have said.
And passion is a wild rank weed,
    a lunge upward of stalks,
      hunting the man, seeds, soil.
Passion *is* a flower; they say right.
And passion is a tough climb out of loam
    with toil, oaths, joy, memory of
      a struggle up.

       . .
       . .

He is a fantastic battler.
He hits, ducks, hits.
Nothing meets his fist where he hits.
Nothing hits at him when he ducks.
He battles phantoms.
Pity the fantasy of him.
Pity yourself and where you came from.
Take this mirror; take a look at yourself.

       . .
       . .

They made such pictures.
There was no end of their sketches.
They were artists.
They had plans; art for art's sake.
They had beauty figured out cold, sure.
The prize word of their mouths was Beauty.
They spelled Beauty with a capital B—
    just like that.

They gave themselves presents, they told each
        other of their excellences, of form, harmony,
        organic truths.
Jehosophat! how they enjoyed their little vocabularies!

                    . .
                    . .

You were made for joy, child.
The feet of you were carved for that.
The ankles of you run for that.
The rise of rain, the shift of the wind,
        the drop of a red star on a far water
        rim—
An endless catalogue of shouts, laughters,
        silent contemplations—
they made you from day to day—for joy—child.

Well, he sat up and said to himself,
"This is good, I will go to it."
Till then he had been satisfied with himself.
Now there came back an old unrest
Carried over from a grandfather as was,
The one grandfather he had failed to live up to.
He had a hunch; a new hunch; another and another;
        instead of ideas, whims, now he had hunches.
So he said, "This is good, I will go to it."

Where is my wandering boy tonight?
Many a mother has asked that as a habit.
They put you in jail.
What good did it do 'em?
You walked out of their jail.
The shackles dropped off you.
They couldn't see your tall wings.
They couldn't feel the fire-mist of you.

When they were proud of their jail—
You said oh-oh, oh-oh, so soft they couldn't
        get the syllables.
There are high magnificent barriers in these
        our simple lives.
There are little words on pale lips it is
        useless to look up in the big books.

Sweet mother, stand and look.
These are your little ones in the moon.
They came out of you to be here,
To be slanted over with flooding, moon silver.
The path of this nocturne leads anywhere.
The moon is a fortune teller; it coaxes, cajoles
        us, tells us what we want to be, so, fools us.
Sweet mother, God be good to you, when you tell
        them how the ladders of life collapse and new
        ladders arise.
Let the print of this moon night be always swept
        on their little mouths.
They came out of you to be here; they go the way
        of ordered numbers.

Dixie Flyer

On the path of the Dixie Flyer
Along two hundred miles on a Sunday afternoon
Wild azalea sprang up and sang, sat up with its
     soft pink leaves.

The path of the Dixie Flyer
Took three curves in Tennessee, in Alabama,
     in Georgia—
The wild azalea was always there.

Buttercups were a yellow rain,
Johnny-jump-ups a blue mist—
The wild azalea sprang a low cry.

The towns ran by, clean towns with big streets,
     dirty towns with little stinking streets
And the old people were coming home from church
     and the children with their faces washed
     were coming home from Sunday school,
And the azaleas two hundred miles that Sunday
     afternoon sprang a low cry.

And all along was a red lantern such as a dark blood
     and a red rest might leave.

What kind of flowers were there flung through the
     weave of those two Tennessee girls at
     Tullalurna?
They stood in their feet tracks waiting for the
     train to go by, yes, they stood still, and
     their bodies danced in windflower rhythms.
The laughter of their eyes came out like flowers,
     thru yellow buttercup rain, thru johnny-jump-up
     blue mist.
The Dixie Flyer flew by Tullahoma

Out along passes where the wild azalea sprang a low cry.
The wild azalea was always there.

Lookout Mountain lays a long shadow across Chattanooga.
Places where men lay lost, lay in wounds in rain,
          lay calling for mothers, water, Christ, lay
          in salt and blood—
Places where trees were born and the spears of grass
          were a spatter of red—
Lookout Mountain lays a long shadow across Chattanooga.

(Grant and Lee are strictly short names.
Grant and Lee were solemn men.
Out of the salt and iron of the earth
          came Grant and Lee.)

The Dixie Flyer crosses Chickamauga Creek—the
          yellow Chickamauga and its green tree shadows
          winds under.
More than one green stream dappled with red blood
          runs to the sea.
On the backwashes and the flat waters on a Sunday
          afternoon in April, an Easter Sunday, the shrilling
          of the frogs rises to a swell.

Li Po, if a village sits by the big bend of the Tennessee
          River fifty years or a thousand years—it is
          still a village.
In a thousand years the fading leaves of its fires
          burn with other stories.
Oothcaloga Creek, can the mockers and the orioles
          call its name?
Does the mourning dove toss its syllables!

Bird Cries and Burnt Flowers

When I heard you singing
the answer to my singing
I knew one hill bird's call
to another hill bird.

    When I heard you singing
    I forgot the desperate,
    I forgot the goose cry,
    the wing whirr late in grey,
    late in the last of dusk.

When I heard you singing
I saw the burnt flowers,
I counted the leaves dying clean,
I sifted the ashes of two poppies,
I saw two flamingoes in Florida sunsets.

    When I heard you singing
    I fathomed a blue flower,
    I measured a bee path in blossoms,
    The kiss of circle and zigzag.

    When I heard you singing
    I remembered the hips of dawn.
    I mentioned the blue egg spots,
    Fluff in the white spring wind
    And all our driven beginnings.
The goose cry again over the burnt flowers
And again and again two flamingoes in Florida sunsets.

Cool May Night

What yellow throat of a tree
sang old things it remembered
and new things it hoped?

What tawny head looked from a tree-top
with a day lantern of color making a soft spot
on the woodland's darker, heavier coat?

Why did a line of thornapple trees
sit in a gray cluster under the yellow throat,
under the tawny head?

Early spring—
Why was the fire and dew of it all
spoken in your eyes and voice?

Malinda

Malinda kept away from sin.
In the places of men's foregathering
None told a sin of Malinda.
. . . Malinda came from Bryn Mawr
   Clean, singing, willowy,
   Malinda etched by the passing years.
What are they saying now
Of the sins of Malinda
Who never sinned?
. . . Malinda is a thing with peach dust on.
   Malinda is perfect and nothing is brought
   Against her, only the sin she never sinned.
Bryn Mawr was golden blue, a horizon,
Bryn Mawr and its sin-never, sin-never,
Bryn Mawr and its well-kept lawns
Out of the aching wilderness grassroots.
. . . So a clean and a singing willowy girl
   Asks of the passing etching years:
   What are they saying now
   Of the sins of Malinda
   Who never sinned?

Old Star and Younger

In a valley where the sun and the rain
      are kind and thoughtful, where they
      never forget—
A mother sleeps in a four-post bed, in white
      sheets, with a new born baby—
And heartbeats of the mother and the baby
      go on under the ribs as if they belong
      in the orbits of two stars, an older and
      a younger star.
And a sorrel cow in the barn sleeps on yellow
      straw with a new calf—and a bluejay
      sleeps high in a maple tree crotch with
      a wet fuzzy one fresh from the broken
      egg shells—and a gray squirrel sleeps
      in a hole in a dry rot stump with a
      blinking, breathing baby gray squirrel—
      and the cow, the blue jay, the gray squirrel
      blink and breathe—
And the heartbeats of the mother and the
      baby go on under the ribs as if they be-
      long in the orbits of two stars, an older
      and a younger star.

Pasture Corner

Now again it may be
a blue star on a lemon sky,
many stars in nets of hair,
tangles of wind branches,
a sickle moon in a sycamore,
star points in a pond scum,
two cows in a pasture corner
serene as the sickle moon—
it may be again,
this little night testament.

Bird Haunted

Always these birds haunt me.
A redbird whose scarlet signature of wings flashes
        against green branches—
A bluebird whose crying purple performs scrolls of
        flight in a winter beech tree.
Branches, beeches, did you see and hear these crooners?

A Wanted Child Is Born

Speak to the windows tonight.
Tell them be heavy, be dim, be hoarse,
with moving of fog and humps of sea,
with shadows and shapes foreshadowing.
The sea is a home and has its own
                                            homeseekers.

Speak to the windows this morning.
Tell them be lighted, be singing,
be sea warm, rain warm, word warm.
Light into color, color into shadow,
shadow into nothing, nothing into
newfound prisms.

Be sure and speak to the windows.
Say you yes you to the windows.

        Birds into a window
        and birds out again
        birds beyond counting—
They fly into films of morning,
They vanish in evening roselight,
They lose themselves in the sea.

        In any room of heavy windows,
        In any house of highlight moments,
        ecstasy is a thinwrought child
        saying you yes you.

        She drew the little one in
        warm in a woven rose-leaf fold,
        sea warm, rain warm, word warm,
        pink as the hearts of melons,
        stranger than white sea-horses—
        thinwrought and crying you yes you.

Good Babies Make Good Poems

Doctor Williams having delivered
eleven hundred babies
in Rutherford New Jersey
also delivered from himself
eleven hundred poems
each poem a baby
to grow up and please the Doctor
and give him pride in himself
as the mother of each baby
and himself her obstetrician
thus having two prides
ever pleasing his heart—
one the embryo poem
in his fertile brain-womb—
the other his obstetric skill
with no use of forceps
delivering the brain-child
to wriggle in black ink on white paper
Doctor Williams saying often to himself,
     "Good babies make good poems."

Advice to a Rare Sweet Child

Let many lights spring forth on the sea for her.
Let the landpaths have many living crosslights.
Let her linger in seafog and read horizons.

The mystery of the sea
has a sister in her.
        The study of love requires a seatalk.
        How deep lies the seabottom?
        Who told the seabirds how to travel?
        What are the measures of bitter waters?
        Does the sea be clumsy and gamble
                for gain or the passion of chance?

Always is a music to be sought out.
In the wood of a chair, a clothespin, an axhandle, a violin.
In the clink of ice on porcelain
Or the ring of a goldpiece on brass
In the travel and twist of lights in a globe of glass
                                long moments all glass.

Zinnia Sonata

For Karlen Paula and John Carl

I have seen zinnias give out
with little songs and begging pardon
for the songs being short.
I have seen zinnias claim their rights
to speak promises   saying to beholders,
     "Whatever may be your wish, sir or madam,
     I promise you shall have it—today, tomorrow,
     somewhere over the blue hills and bright valleys,
     it shall be yours to keep—whatever you wish—
     we so promise—we zinnias God made for promising."
I have heard zinnias counseling together:
     "Ever the summer is kind to us,
     summer belonging to us as we belong to summer.
     When God said, 'Let there be summer'
     He also said, 'And let there be zinnias
     bathed in colors called from sunsets and early stars.'
     And God having so spoken
     how can we be either proud or humble?
     how can we be aught else than quiet blooming zinnias?"

        Thus having heard the zinnias
        I shall go again and again to hear the zinnias.

Sky Promises

Sometimes you seem to be made of white moon stuff
or again you are composed of many light blossoms
mist blossoms moving in a spring wind
    yet this tells nothing of your flying storms
when you riding a big broom in the sky
speak to the storms ordering them where to go
    so you keep in your head and heart many people
the wise young ones who talk with the sky
understanding what the blue sky talks back to them
giving the sky big promises
and hearing the sky come back with bigger promises
these you hold in you while you hold still others
elders   sad ones   thorns alive in their bosoms
wanderers with nails aching in their hearts
    so many people live and move in you
    I love all your living moving people
and best I love your white-moon light-blossom people

Different Moons for Different Children
For John Carl and Karlen Paula

A dish of moving light
skims over the sky—
is this your moon?

Have you seen smoke and
cloud come over the moon
yet later
it looks washed and wiped?

Could it be a big bright penny
one night in a wild wind
got lost up in the sky—
        got lost and then found?

The new moon, baby moon,
sings low, sings bye-lo, bye-lo,
sings soft as a cradle moon.

        The fingernail moon,
        a sliver of cheese,
        silver canoe, crescent,
        you can have them,
        yours to take home,
        yours to keep floating
        in the keeps of your head.

        Have you seen the harvest
        moon grin "Howdy howdy"?
        Or the half-moon saying
        half a "Yes," half a "No"?
        And does the lonesome moon
        tell the lonesome child:
            "Me too, me too"?

Does the frosted moon feel chilly?
Have you watched it shake and shiver?
    Could the moon be
a silver dollar for you to spend
or maybe a new looking-glass
    for you to fly high
    to find your face in it?

Peeping moons
    slide out from clouds,
    peep a while
        and then slide back.

The rising moon comes slow
asking you to try your hand
at pushing it back and down
            where it came from,
            laughing a little:
            "Somehow I do this
            always the same way."

What is it
        the late setting moon
            seems to say?
            "I forgot something
            and I'll be back
        when I remember what it was."

And all these moons
so different from each other
        belong to you,
each moon strictly personal
        and staying in the sky
for you to come back to it.

And whichever moon you love best
says, "Take me home with you.
      If your song is lonesome
      take me home with you."

Second Sonata for Karlen Paula

Could the calm of the sea today
    or the storm of the sea tomorrow
    be held in one drop of water—
    peace today, anger tomorrow,
    in one drop of water?

            Could you be calm today
            and tomorrow be a storm
            and so yourself be
            maybe the sea yesterday
            maybe one drop of water today?

     If among archangels or archdemons
        one knows you and loves you
        could you speak to it
        late every evening saying,
    "Remember me—every evening remember me"??

        Try standing in the sun, telling your shadow,
        "I like you much—you never fail me."
Begin with zero, naught, nothing.
Count ten and find the numbers
all here today the same as yesterday.
        Can you look where anger has spilled and
        splashed and then consult all your angers
        from A to Z?

     Be jungle dark in your heart
     and then find the black moonlight
     of a silence holding your soft voice:
     "Sleep and peace always wash my heart."

        Study the wingbone of a dry dead bird—
            how light it was for flying!
Look easy at the knee-joint of a goat skeleton—
     how it could summon a leap from rock to rock!

Contemplate a rose gone to ashes—
and the perfect dignity of ashes!

When you watch a gold half-moon
scud from out one silver cloud
to move into another silver cloud
you may find yourself whispering:
"You scud and I scud—from moment to moment
we both scud."

Looking at a tall elm swaying in a storm-wind
you may find yourself saying: "I honor, Oh Tree,
I honor the deep roots unseen underground
holding you seen overground."

June 28, 1953

Loon

A loon in a moon, far north in a Canada moon, a loon:
   "Ask me anything."
And they asked him, the loon in the moon, far north in
   a Canada moon, they asked him, "What is money, love,
   fame, contentment, power?"
And the loon let out a loud wail and came across: "Money
   is a monkey with many coconuts—love is a morsel over
   a slow fire—fame is a firefly for fish who yearn—
   contentment is the irreducible minimum of hankerings—
   power is a hunk of mud wanting the moon for the author-
   ity it lends."

Name on the Air

I will write my name to hang in the air
hoping the hang of it in the air will please me
till a wind comes picking each vowel and consonant,
setting them to roost with birds on branches,
while I walk under them saying:
The sun and the rain are
                 two of my great-great-grandmothers,
                 two of my youngest sisters.

Instructions to Whatever Gardens

I have left the sunflowers,
Wild grape, trumpet vine—
What is more, I have left dahlias—
I have left zinnias, asters, white tobacco
    blossoms opening to dusk and dawn.
I have left tomatoes and rows of corn,
The song of crabapples falling to the ground.
I have left airy songs in and out of all these
    stalks and vines.
Cut the blossoms, pick the fruits, eat them, give them away,
But don't let the seeds drift off on the winds with the songs—
And I have left even more beautiful words
    twisted among the roots, deep down—
When you hoe, when you weed
Don't break the delicate bitter roots or
    You will break our favorite songs.

Accept Your Face with Serious Thanks

Grief is one of the great known etchers.
Sorrow is a writer on faces.
Meet these half-way and see what happens.
Accept your face with serious thanks.
The silence of a sad face has ten values.
The lips of a clown are not sad for nothing.
To go down and under and out for the last time
Is to meet many others merged in dust.
Have a sad face willing to be so.
Study the wilderness under your own hat
And say little or nothing of how
You are not unaccustomed to thorns.

Pastoral

Love is a sweet bird to be thinking about
when labor is a heavy going.

Joy is a gong to be heard
when good work comes to a fine point.

    Death rots slowly
    those who have nothing to do
    and know not how to do nothing.

Bubble

Come and give us hope:
    Pictures come to our eyes
    And songs arrive at our ears
    And the tears well and our hearts shake:
Yet a moment and it is all over
And we laugh at the world for ashes—
A bubble God blew one day
And then shaped little philosophers
To make Him merry in
A running to and fro with explanations
Of How and Why
The bubble is a bubble.

Poppy Leaf

The moments of a poppy leaf
slowly unfolding in the sun
and meeting rain and wind
make a pageless diary
of a grand pageless book—
and one red bookmark—
one crimson marginal note—
lost in the leaves of fall.

How Long Ago Was All This?

How long ago was it
when I was a glockenspiel
in a time faded to a dusty whisper?
    Then too I was a libretto
    with clefs and bars clean scriven
    and I became a lost script
    crumpled and eaten beyond reading—
    mice got me before singers saw me.
Before I was a bell I was a drum.
Before I was a drum I was a clock.
Can anyone now tell me the time?
              How long ago was all this?

Galuppi

Galuppi in a garret wrote a toccata,
Saying to casual callers, "This,"
Meaning thereby the little room
With little windows reached by climbing stairs,
"This is where I dirty paper."
There he spatters black ink on white reams,
flinging runs, slurs, arpeggios up and down
the five-step ladder—each note a little bird
   he tells where to sit.

· ·

   Let me chisel a few prayers.
   Let me print a few dots of song.
   Let me make one strong silence.
   Let me keep a hard name.
   Let me go as the air of grey wind goes.

· ·

"Dear dead women," said one of the toccata,
"What's become of all the gold used to hang
and brush their bosoms?"

He was an anxious Englishman and sang his anxiety.
He too had places where he dirtied paper—
A banker's home in England, a villa in Italy.

· ·

Give me a quiet garret alone
Where I may sit for a few casual callers
And tell them carelessly, offhandedly,
"This is where I dirty paper."

Thus each poet prays and dreams.
The eternal hobo asks for a quiet room
   with a little paper he can dirty,
     with birds who sit where he tells 'em.

Mr. Blake's Chariots

Mr. Blake saw invisible chariots on the sky
driven by unseen charioteers.
Himself he saw as a slim wisp of an ashen
mortality
And nevertheless took himself for a charioteer
riding high, grand and lonely.

Even Shakespeare

Even Shakespeare must have said to himself,
"I have her kisses even though we never kiss again."
And having said so to himself then making an acknowledgment
Other Englishmen, Scandinavian sea captains, Spanish freebooters,
Italian window makers and Arabian camel drivers,
Often said each one of them to himself,
"I have her kisses even though we never kiss again."
Looking idly at the march of starlit meadows,
His heels only a moment away from a dark-eyed woman's doorstep,
Shakespeare must have said so to himself.

Study in Rock Color

Six writers of dreams
Beat their heads on sea-rocks
And kept on writing dreams
Out of their heads,
Out of the sea-rocks.

Frozen red of the sea-rocks,
Frozen roar of the headlands,
Kept on in the six writings of dreams.

Topstone

Sometimes old men sitting near
the exits of life say, "There were
giants in those days."
They wanted stones to sit on,
stones to throw at each other,
great stones for companions,
for loneliness, all giants being
lonely.

Fingal

The meditations of many years
weigh down his head.
He and his kith and kin have seen
too many wolves to be happy all
the time.
So he lays his great head on his long
paws—and thinks—and thinks—
for hours.

Wild Thornapple Tree

The wild thornapple tree fastens its roots deep
and twists into the soil so the wind has hard
work loosening it.

In the winter the wild thornapple tree has
a welcome for the white snowdrifts
maneuvering and shifting.

In the spring the wild thornapple tree
cries with soft blossoms
and lets fall a May snow of its own.

On Windy Thursday Evenings

Little steeples of tiny wooden churches in Massachusetts,
Sometimes you point straight at the moon the same as a
        child's finger saying to another child, "There it
        is, I can find the moon for you if there is a moon
        to find."
We have all seen this on windy Thursday evenings—a moon—
        —a high gold plate God sent sailing through the
        sky on windy Thursday evenings.
The moon lets the wind blow it till it is exactly over the
        little steeples of small wooden Massachusetts churches.
Then it is identified, then the moon stops and says, "There, little
        steeples, wooden cross churches are pointing straight
        at me—same as children's fingers."
Yes, this happens on windy Thursday evenings.

There Are Great Loves

There are great loves like great walnut trees.
The roots take long to grow and the branches live on and take size and reach out
And make at last a pictorial memory in a strong masterpiece of landscapes.
And every root, child, counts on one combat after another, every branch counts on one combat after another, the days and years are a series of gnarled combats.
There is one struggle with the hot suns and there is another struggle when the rains are too many or two few—there is a fight one year with fire and another year with water.
There are thwarted roots, branches given up and gone, feeders and feelers dying on the way, wasted leaf or limb whose profile rots against a dumb sky of short months.
And the tree takes hold and grows, root and branch lengthen and fasten, and the tree groans in the lonesome monotones, and the tree groans in wrestling repeated storm winds, "God, it goes slow"—so the walnut tree takes hold and grows.
So might a great love take hold and wonder and grow, so might a great love out of an idle Tuesday take hold and groan out of its combats and the lonesome monotones, so might a great love at last be a pictorial memory in a strong masterpiece.
So might a great love or a great language or a great walnut tree pass along the idle disk of time and leave its short thumbprint on the high blue walls of time's sky.
So I have seen five or six take hold and wonder and groan and grow— so I have seen root and leaf and branch fail and wither with their profiles.

Concerto Fragment

The sunset made a soft music
of pink doors closing one by one
inviting nightsongs along the west
beckoning shafts and handles of stars
bringing folds of moonmist curtains.

* *

The flame rose may be a flower given.
Sorrow may come after as a garment worn.
The warm, the hungering, seek bread and blossom.
The lost and sunken understand perfect quiet.
Tidepools swarm with the eaters and the eaten.
The not-so-strong go down before the stronger.
Love may beget a mess of serpents
                              or a whirl of white birds.
Love may beget a living wall of wine-dark roses
                              or a little pile of cold ashes.

Guessers

Old man Euclid had 'em guessing.
He let the wise guys laugh and went his way.
Planes, solids, rhomboids, polygons—
Signs and cosines—
He had their number,
Even the division of a circle's circumference
     by its diameter never fazed him—
It was Pi to him.

Galileo told 'em something.
"You're nuts," they said, "you for the padded cell,
     you for the booby hatch
     and the squirrel cage."
"Have your laugh," he answered.
"Have your laugh and let it ride.
     Let it ride . . . for a thousand years or so."

Newton let 'em grin and giggle.
He smiled when they chuckled, "Nobody home."
He looked 'em over
     and went on listening to damsons, listening
     to autumn apples falling with their "now you
     see it, now you don't."
"Maybe," is all he told 'em, "perhaps is all the
     answer . . . perhaps and . . . who knows . . .
     in a thousand years."

And now, bo, here's this Einstein;
Good for a laugh in all the funny sections.
Sure-fire stuff in the movies, comic-operas,
     burlesque, jazz parlors, honky tonks,
     two-a-day.

Somebody asks him "How about Euclid? . . .
      Was he all twisted? . . . And is it true
      your kink in space will put the kibosh
      on Copernicus?"
Einstein looks 'em over and tells 'em "Maybe
. . . and then again . . . perhaps."
He says "The truth is all—supposing . . . the
      truth is all . . . come back and ask me . . .
      in a thousand years."

Evidence As to a She Devil

Socrates had a fool woman.
She ragged him, nagged him.
Her initial was X for Xantippe.
Socrates learned about women from her.
She was a shrew, a virago, a hell cat.
        So they say.
        So-they-say.
What we know is what they say.
We do not know what Xantippe would reply
If asked, why did you rag and nag Socrates?
She might say he was lousy and bring evidence.
She might lie till we saw she was a regular liar.
She might show him as lazy, gabby, no provider.
Or she might hurl many furious useless words
Till she sounded like a leather-tongued scold.
We know only what they say.
        We have not heard from Xantippe herself.

Contemplation Basket

A flamewash swim of five scarlet fish
gives eyes a deed of motion and light.

One fast line of a redbird flight
can hold the heart of a sunrise cry.

A basket of yellow corn,
a bowl of black-and-gold pansies,
may feed hungering blood and thirsting eyes.

The slide of a spotted snake to a slant of sun
or the flagrance of the June bloom of peonies
or the laughter of a bushel of new potatoes—
they may speak to the eyes and the blood.

The hushed rituals of gold and shadow
move over summer oats, over harvest corn,
measuring seasons with silent feet and fingers.

* *

Anguish may come as a fierce garment.
Ecstasy too is a relentless vesture.
Each arrives unbidden in a criss-cross.

* *

The shape of water adjusts itself
to the form of land under and around it.

The slide of a white fluff of cloud
gives over to whatever wind
comes shoving from whichever way.

All doors give way and open
in accord with proper keys brought.

* *

Does the hoarse sea have salt for a purpose?
Does the white moon have shape toward an end?
Does the big night tent of stars come on an errand?
Do lesser or larger magnets move to an ordered music?
Have conversations of the sea and the moon been overheard
or the triple talk of sun, sky, and rainbow
    or the dawn speech of night and morning
                        day and evening
                            at parting hours?

* *

If—We Are Met Up

If you have turned a door knob
and felt the knob at your fingers
turn and keep turning
till its turnings told you
the knob was out of connection
and the lock and the hinges
only laughed at the useless knob—
I shall be glad—we are met up.

If you felt along a wall for a clock
and after your fingers found the clock
you lighted a match to see the time
and the clock showed you its face
and the twelve numbers of the hours were there
and the pendulum was swinging sure as a gallows
death watch while the sound of a tick-tock
went on—and all you needed to read the time
was an hour hand and a minute hand
on the face of the clock—
I shall be glad—we are met up.

Thistledown and Brass

If hell is deeper, as they say, than the sea,
If heaven is higher, as they also declare, than the sky,
Then the laughter of a poppy or a bluebell may be mentioned
And the scarf of a miracle stitched in scarlet.

    If thistledown may blend with five gongs in a rain
    Then midnight has thongs no less than morning
    And time is a roan horse for moon shooters.
The metaphor of a mustang foot and ribs may operate;
    Joints and thews made to fling heels at the stars.

    And what causes impel flamingoes?
Above webfoot bottoms rise perpendicular legs.
Fine then are the feathers to sheathe a torso in a pink sheen.
    In the crescendo is lifted an interrogatory neck
    And eyes putting only pink flamingo queries.

    Brass may be laid upon an anvil.
Hammers may dent unconscionable laughter on it.
Or the repercussions of handlers may smooth brass
Till it mirrors seven hoarse circles of grackles
    each in a robe of violet shadow feathers,
Till it forms a pool of dwarfs climbing miniature
    staircases to a moon of changing numbers,
Till it brings into one room thistledown thongs
    flamingoes five gongs in a rain.

When War Is in Their Hearts

When fear is in their minds,
When pride is woven in the will,
When war is in their hearts,
When they know what they want
And they want their pride kept,
Then, gentlemen, the war will come.

  Can books help?
  Can music or meditation help?
  Can the high givers wearing insignia
  bring us no more than wornout words
  heard over, heard often,
  heard till they slide away
  and keep nowhere any sacred corners?

  How long will the new weapons be new?
  Will they be new when the war comes?
  How far shall the trust be put
  in today's weapons surpassing yesterday's?
  And shall this be done in the name
  and as before over and over and over
    of Christ and the Christian Society?

Chapters

I Remember me with little nothings.
    Bring me no handfuls anyone would buy.
    Bring me nothing called for in the lists
        or the memoranda of things to be wrapped
        in packages and delivered.
    Send me envelopes from nowhere kissed
        on the flaps with a hint of your finger-
        prints, your tongue, your breath on it.

II Kiss me once for every day and once for
        every hour
    We will be gone from each other.
    Kiss me once for each collected passion to come,
        once for every gnawing insistent longing,
        once for every wild wish to be taken and swept
        like a leaf in the wind.

III And so . . we must be going
    And so . . this is all.
        Winter will march its armies up and down.
        Spring will come again and sing like a little
            girl meeting its first passion.
        Summer will follow with its laughing roots and
            climbing leaves.
        Autumn will let loose its old mockeries and
            spin new webs of harvest.
        And this is all . . has nothing to do with us . .
            because we are through . . we must be going . .
            this is all . . it is over.

Notes

OTHERS. This was written especially for the little poetry magazine *Others,* and was given to the publisher, Alfred Kreymborg, on his visit to the Sandburg home in Maywood, Illinois. It was published in the July, 1916 issue.

FROM AN ILLINOIS PRAIRIE HUT. This was originally titled "Three Notations on the Visit of a Massachusetts Woman to the House of Neighbors in Illinois." Amy Lowell wrote Sandburg that she liked it even if she never did live in Vermont. She particularly liked the last line.

PORTRAIT OF A COLYUMNIST. The "colyumnist" is Tub Hedrick of the Chicago *Daily News,* and the column was called "Orientations of Ho-Hum." It consisted of "hokkus" signed with outrageous pseudo-nyms that were much enjoyed by his readers: Igetcha Nau, Kilthiah Umpiah, Kumesi Goesi, Osakanu See.

SOJOURNER TRUTH SPEAKING. Sojourner Truth was an ex-slave who spoke against slavery in the time of Lincoln. She met Lincoln at the age of eighty.

TOPSTONE. Topstone is the name of the great rock across the lake from Edward Steichen's home, which is called Umpawaug. The "old men" of course are Sandburg and Steichen, both of whom liked the idea of great stones as companions, and "stones to throw at each other" is an allusion to the continual jibing that went on between the two.